It snowed in L_____ _____
day, but it didn'_____ ____
was to be a fight between the Russian champion and the American champion. Everyone wanted to see it.

Suddenly the crowd was on its feet, booing and whistling. Rocky walked down the aisle toward the ring. The boos gave way to jeers and crude gestures, but Rocky walked through the crowd, his eyes straight ahead.

Then the arena erupted into more noise, but this time it was cheering. Drago, the Russian champ, walked down the opposite aisle. The crowd went wild, a tidal wave of noise: Drago! Drago! Drago! Drago!

Rocky bounced up and down on the balls of his feet, his eyes never leaving the Russian....

A ROBERT CHARTOFF - IRWIN WINKLER Production

"ROCKY IV"

Starring SYLVESTER STALLONE

TALIA SHIRE · BURT YOUNG

CARL WEATHERS · BRIGITTE NIELSEN

DOLPH LUNDGREN as Drago

Music Composed by VINCE DiCOLA

Director of Photography BILL BUTLER, ASC

Executive Producers JAMES D. BRUBAKER and ARTHUR CHOBANIAN

Produced by IRWIN WINKLER and ROBERT CHARTOFF

Written and Directed by SYLVESTER STALLONE

# ROCKY IV

## SYLVESTER STALLONE

BALLANTINE BOOKS • NEW YORK

Library of Congress Catalog Card Number: 85–90760

ISBN 0-345-32849-3

Manufactured in the United States of America

First Edition: November 1985

# Prologue

The spray from the shower head drummed incessantly on Rocky's head. He didn't mind it; in fact, he welcomed it. It made him oblivious to everything, even to Apollo Creed standing in the next shower cubicle. It was finally over. He had paid his debt to Apollo. They had had their rematch and now they were even. There had been no loser, no winner, just two friends, tired and contented. Rocky turned his head and a blast of water stung his red, swollen left eye. He winced in pain. It snapped him out of his mindless reverie. He was glad that Apollo hadn't been able to see the wince, but he would have understood it. Pain was a part of their lives. Pain was a part of boxing. Boxing. Boxing. It all came back to boxing. For better or for worse he felt he had gone through most of his life with boxing gloves on. It had made for tenuous handholds. The water continued to soothe him, lulling him into a sleeplike trance. The sound of the cascading water increased to a roar.

The crowd roared as the bell rang to signal the end of the round. Clubber continued to pound Rocky. The referee bulled his way in and separated the two fighters. The cheers and boos of the crowd became a continuous electrical humming in the back of Rocky's head.

He walked wearily to his corner.

Apollo angrily grabbed Rocky by the shoulders.

"What the hell are you doing?"

"I know what I'm doing."

"If you stand toe-to-toe with him, you've lost, understand? He's too strong. He'll kill you. Box him damn it!" Apollo said tensely, pushing Rocky down on the stool.

"He's getting tired," Rocky said stoically.

Donut, Clubber's manager, wiped his fighter's face off. A small trickle of blood still oozed from the nose, but it was nothing serious. The eyes were still undamaged.

"Don't go wastin' ya punches. He's got nothin' left," Donut encouraged.

"Nothin'!" Clubber growled, his eyes glaring across the ring at Rocky.

"You're the champ. You take him out this round!"

"He's mine," Clubber said ominously. "He's mine."

Apollo paced angrily in front of Rocky.

"If you trade with him, he'll kill you—just keep moving side to side and using the left lead. You've got to try! Hey, you came here to win this fight—*win* it! Eye of the tiger, damn it! Eye of the tiger!"

The buzzer sounded. Rocky stood.

Adrian watched him, horrified yet spellbound.

Clubber loomed in his corner like an immense tower.

"Wear him down," Donut yelled. "He's all ours."

The bell rang.

Round three.

"Here we are in the third round of this already incredibly grueling contest that should logically never have gone beyond round two. The bell sounds and Clubber rushes to continue his ruthless body attack on the former champion," the commentator yelled into the microphone, his face turning pink from exertion. He felt himself wearing down like the fighters in the ring.

Clubber exploded out of his corner, intent on finishing Rocky for good. Rocky backpedaled, diffusing the attack, even countering with some jabs that successfully kept Clubber at bay.

"Five quick jabs in Clubber's face. The champion brushes them aside and chases Balboa down. Oh, a solid hook drives Rocky into his own corner—this could be all she wrote," the commentator continued.

Rocky huddled in his corner as Clubber unleashed a barrage of devastating blows. Rocky felt like a ship being pounded in a storm. Every way he turned he was pummeled. There was no safe harbor in this ring.

"It's all over now. The champion is landing blows at will. This fight could be over—No! Balboa slips and blocks. Triple hooks by Balboa have stunned the champion. Here comes Rocky!"

Rocky blocked two powerful rights and landed a beautiful series of hooks on Clubber's head. The blood from the cuts around Rocky's eyes was tinting his world pink, an almost-peaceful, rosy hue. Clubber stumbled back, jarred and shaken. Rocky jumped forward, connecting with a rapid series of body punches. Clubber continued to back up, suddenly in trouble. Rocky stalked him, continually ripping and tearing at his body. Rocky's gloves were a brown blur.

Hysteria swept over the crowd.

Adrian was on her feet, chanting "Rocky! Rocky!"

Now it was Rocky's turn. He blasted Clubber's body with hooks alternated with combinations to the head. Clubber was in agony. His arms had lost all feeling. One of his ribs felt broken. But he would not go down. He was a champion!

A tremendous right drove Clubber into the ropes.

Paulie jumped up and down in Rocky's corner, pulling at his hat and chewing his forgotten cigar.

"Break his head! Break everything!"

The commentator leaned forward expectantly. "Rocky is back, burying his fist in Lang's face, then switching to caving in the champion's ribs. An incredible comeback. No, wait—Rocky is hurt!"

Clubber ducked under an arching left and ripped an uppercut to the liver that paralyzed Rocky's body. It was the most exquisite pain Rocky had ever felt. His body seemed to melt into slow motion. Clubber waded in and mutilated Rocky with pile-driving head and body shots and then drove him across the ring in a complete reverse of the previous action. It looked hopeless for Rocky.

The crowd was standing now, chanting "Rocky! Rocky!" The sound swept through the arena like a mantra.

Adrian stood, too, but her eyes were closed and she

3

was silent. She was praying.

Paulie pounded the canvas with his fist. "Go after him! Tear him up!"

Suddenly Rocky cut loose with a flurry of hooks that caught the champion by surprise and sent him reeling against the ropes. Rocky moved to the center of the ring. Gesturing with his gloves, he defiantly urged Clubber to come and get him. A terrible smile slashed Rocky's face as he continued the motion.

"C'mon, c'mon," he yelled at Clubber.

The crowd went wild at the sight of the challenge.

"Look at that!" the commentator urged. "Balboa is challenging the champion to come ahead. I can't believe it."

Paulie leaned down by the commentator. "Believe it," he said. Then he turned his attention back to the ring and yelled, "Get him, Rocko!"

Clubber came off the ropes and waded into Rocky. They stood toe-to-toe, hurling long-armed bombs at each other from point-blank range. Neither man attempted to duck a blow. They were just too tired.

"Balboa with a combination—reply to the head by the champion—it's trench warfare—the old Rocky is back. Oh, the champion is hurt! He is being demolished!"

It was like the old days for Rocky. All thought of style was gone from his head. He didn't feel the blows that landed on him. He concentrated on his old style of bruising infighting. Clubber was being damaged. His hands were slowly being forced down from his face. Finally, Rocky saw an opening and fired a scathing volley of accurate punches to Clubber's head. The champion staggered backwards. He couldn't regain his balance. Rocky pummeled him into a corner.

"Let it loose! Let it loose!" Apollo screamed.

Rocky pulled out all the stops. He tattooed his opponent with three hooks to the body, three rights to the head. Clubber swayed like a building on the brink of collapse. Rocky whipped a murderous right hook. The building crashed; Clubber toppled sideways.

Rocky leapt to a neutral corner; the referee began his count over the prostrate champion.

The crowd rocked the arena with deafening cheers. People turned and hugged one another.

4

Adrian looked at Rocky. He was staring at her, his eyes wild as an animal's in the heat of battle.

"Get up! Get up!" Donut yelled in a frenzy from Clubber's corner.

But Clubber didn't even know which way was up. His body felt as if it were made of jelly instead of muscle.

Apollo and Paulie were in suspended animation watching the referee's count.

"Six. Seven. Eight. Nine. Ten! You're out!"

The arena exploded like midnight on New Year's Eve. People swarmed wildly into the aisles, jumping and dancing. There was so much paper flying through the air it looked like a ticker tape parade. The ring was flooded by reporters and well-wishers.

Rocky leapt into the air and landed in Apollo's embrace.

"You did it, man! You've got nothing to prove to nobody! Nothing!" Apollo cried as he hugged Rocky.

The ring announcer was shouting to make himself heard above the general din. "Winner by a knockout, in one of the most incredible comebacks in boxing history."

Adrian was suddenly in Rocky's arms, smothering him with kisses. He didn't know how she had managed to fight her way through the crowd, but he didn't care. All he wanted to do was kiss her and hold her.

"It's all over," Rocky whispered to her.

"How do you feel?" she asked, looking at his battered face.

"And once again the heavyweight champion of the world, the pride of Philadelphia, Rocky Balboa!"

"Never better. Never better," Rocky murmured as he kissed her again and again.


But it hadn't been completely over. There was still the favor to Apollo.

The water from the shower collected around his feet and swirled down the rusty drain. Rocky heard Apollo turn off the shower in the cubicle beside him.

The favor. In all the time Rocky had known Apollo Creed he had never completely understood him. He had been in awe of him, marveled at him, fought him, been beaten by him, beaten him, but never understood him. There was only one Apollo. He was complex and unique. The favor was not really a surprise because anything that comes from a surprising person is bound to be unusual.

They met at Goldmill's gym. It had been closed since Mickey's death. The gym was still, tomblike. Its inhabitants had unhappily dispersed to other gyms around the city, but they weren't the same. There was only one Goldmill's. The dreams of sweat and blood that lingered in the gathering dust of the gym were not transferable.

The old, dented locker doors slammed shut as Rocky and Apollo finished putting on their boxing outfits.

"Y'know, I can't believe you're doing this," Rocky said as they headed out of the locker room.

"We made a deal," Apollo replied.

"Yeah, but this is extremely crazy."

"Yeah, mentally irregular," Apollo agreed.

They walked through the deserted gym to the well-worn ring. A shaft of moonlight shone down through the skylight, illuminating the ring.

Rocky could almost hear the heavy breathing of phantom boxers as they struggled with jump ropes, speed bags, and medicine balls.

"But it makes all the sense it needs to make," Apollo stated. "You owe me a favor, right?"

"Yeah. When'd you think of this?"

"About three years ago."

"This is crazy."

"The last time we met you were lucky, you beat me by one second. Now, that is hard for a man of my intelligence to handle."

"But didn't you say you'd learned to be happy after losing to me?"

Apollo's smile was wide and mischievous. "I lied."

Rocky nodded his head, understanding. "So you just gotta know for yourself."

"Just for myself," Apollo repeated.

Rocky jumped up on the ring canvas, then reached down a helping hand and pulled Apollo up.

"Go slow. You're not as young as springtime no more," Rocky warned.

"Young enough to whip your butt."

"How can you win? You taught me all your tricks."

Apollo laughed. "Not everything."

Rocky smiled. He felt as good as he had the first time he'd put on a pair of gloves years ago.

"Stallion, I want you to remember that you might fight great, but I'm a great fighter. Ready?"

"Absolutely."

They moved to the center of the ring and began circling.

All over the country kids were picking up baseball gloves, adjusting shoulder pads, putting on boxing gloves, getting set to run out the kitchen door in pursuit of excitement, challenges, and victories.

"Too bad we gotta get old, Stallion."

"Just keep punching," Rocky said.

They moved toward each other smiling, their arms cocked and ready. Simultaneously, each unleashed a devastating punch that rocked the other's head.

Rocky and Apollo left Goldmill's gym. The Philadelphia night was clear and crisp, crisp enough for them to feel chilled from their recent showers. Rocky's eye was getting redder by the minute, while one of Apollo's eyes was beginning to puff up like a biscuit in the oven. They looked proudly at each other's wounds. It had been a good workout for both of them.

"Ah! Almost-fresh air!" Apollo sighed.

Rocky, almost as a reflex from his youth, quickly surveyed the street. To his surprise, he saw Duke leaning against Apollo's exotic white Rolls Royce.

"Almost," Rocky said, then he yelled toward the car. "Hey, Duke!"

"How you doing, Champ?" Duke asked, waving nonchalantly.

"Fine, fine. What're you doing out here?"

"Guarding the property," Duke answered, patting the highly polished car.

"Bad neighborhood. Answer one thing," Apollo requested. "Do you have a hammer in your glove?"

"I was gonna ask you the same thing," Rocky answered.

Apollo gave Rocky's eye a closer inspection and broke into a big smile.

"That hurt you as much as mine hurts me?"

"Absolutely!" Rocky assured him.

"That makes me feel a whole lot better. Y'know, I think it's about time we stop damaging each other."

"I agree."

For a moment they just looked at each other, unable

to find the words to express their thoughts. Their lives had been interwoven for years. Together they had experienced highs and lows that nobody else could understand. They were champions, members of a very exclusive club. The silent pause continued until they both started feeling uncomfortable. Finally, Rocky reached out and shook Apollo's hand.

"Hey, Apollo, I wanna say thanks for everything you did. And to me you'll always be the best."

"Well..." Apollo stammered. For once the man who had bamboozled audiences with his magic spiel had to struggle for words. "I'm gonna miss it and I'm gonna miss you."

They both felt weary, drained. Not because of the words, but because they sensed that their world had irrefutably changed.

Rocky suddenly smiled as he stared at Apollo.

"What's funny, Stallion?"

"Nothing much. I just never saw you wearing a hat."

"A hat gives a man's head class. And keeps his brain warm." Apollo took the hat off and tossed it to Rocky. "Maybe you should try it."

Rocky put the hat on, adjusting it this way and that until he was satisfied. He looked at Apollo for approval. "What do you think?"

"Very Italian. Well, we gotta be going before we get mugged out here," Apollo said, laughing.

"Where you going?" Rocky asked.

"I don't know," Apollo said, more to himself than to Rocky. "Somewhere peaceful. The world's getting to be a violent place, Stallion."

His smile was slow and sad as he waved at Rocky and headed toward his car. Rocky watched his receding figure, sensing the end of a boxing era. It was hard for him to imagine Apollo being content as an ex-celebrity.

Duke started the engine. Apollo got in and the car pulled away from the curb. Soon the red taillights vanished in the night.

Rocky turned to take a last look at Goldmill's. It was appropriate that it end here where it had all started. Rocky had been fifteen years old when he first entered the building. Mickey had scowled over his cigar at him and asked his name.

Robert Balboa, but my friends call me Rocky.
Like in Marciano.
Yeah.
We'll see.

Rocky shivered slightly as a cold gust of air whipped through his suit coat, then he turned and walked away.

# Chapter 1

Adrian counted to herself as she sank the last candles into the thick chocolate frosting of the huge birthday cake. Thirty-six, thirty-seven, thirty-eight, thirty-nine, forty. Done. Her fingers were cramping slightly and she massaged them as she surveyed her work. The candles almost obliterated the "Happy Birthday Paulie" on the cake. She wondered if she should have used just one symbolic candle, but quickly dismissed the thought because she realized the value Paulie put on quantity over quality. Besides, it was quite an accomplishment for Paulie to have reached forty. There were a lot of people who would have bet against it.

Rocky Junior rushed through the kitchen door, a portable movie camera with a sun gun on top of it bobbling in his hands.

"Stop running and be careful with that camera," Adrian warned. "It's not a toy. Your father's told you that."

"Where is Dad?" the boy inquired. "Why isn't he here now?"

"He's on his way."

"From where?"

"Somewhere. Now leave me alone and get out of the kitchen."

Rocky Junior ran out of the kitchen.

"And don't run."

But it was too late. The kitchen door was already swinging shut.

Adrian shook her head in wonderment. Was this the tiny seven-pound bundle of pinkness that she had held in her arms almost five years ago? Paulie wasn't the only one getting old. Rocky Junior was over four feet tall and still shooting up as fast as bamboo. It was only a matter of years before he'd be taller than she was. The thought gave her pleasure.

She turned her attention back to the cake. How do you light forty candles? She almost regretted giving the house-keeper the night off. Well, she'd worry about it when Rocky got here.

That was another thing. Where was he?

She looked at her watch. He was definitely late. He had promised to be on time right before he went out the door. He had said something about going to see Apollo.

Where was he?

She wasn't really worried, maybe just concerned.


Paulie gazed at his reflection in the full-length mirror on his closet door. He had been inspecting himself for the last twenty minutes. He'd assume a frontal position, then switch to a profile. The frontal view showed an inner tube around his waist. The side position revealed a medicine ball where his stomach should be.

Forty.

How'd this happen to him? He felt the same as he had when he was a kid. Oh, maybe he was a little slower and got winded a little faster, but that wasn't so bad when you considered that he never had been fast and had always lacked endurance. Come to think of it, he had never been skinny, either.

But he had had hair when he was a kid, thick and dark. Now it was all salt-and-pepper with an occasional spot of pink scalp showing through. Aw, hell, he thought, that's what hats are for. This was just another birthday, nothing to get upset about. In this life you could never go backward, just forward. Forty sure beat a blank.

Disgusted at his childishness, Paulie turned away from the mirror.

A cone-shaped party hat sat on his bed. He'd wear it, but he still thought it looked stupid. Good thing there was

11

just going to be family at the party. He wished Rocky would get home so the party could start. He wanted to find out what his present was. He was hoping for a sports car. The older he got the more help he needed when he tried for a little action.

Yeah, he'd look good behind the steering wheel of a little sports job. Maybe he'd even trade in his porkpie hat for one of those English-looking things with a brim.

Where was Rocky?

After leaving Goldmill's Rocky had gotten into his sleek black sports car and driven around the old neighborhood. He felt confused almost to the point of depression and he didn't know why.

Driving the car helped him put the thought out of his mind. The gears meshed smoothly. The steering had fingertip precision. Rocky was in complete control. Tonight it was very reassuring.

South Street, like everything else, had changed in the last few years. The Blue Door Fight Club had closed and been replaced by a laundry. The empty lots had been turned into small, ugly shopping centers that resembled concrete blocks. Here and there one could still see a secondhand store, but their days were numbered. The Animal Town Pet Shop, where he had first met Adrian, was another casualty. It had been replaced by a bar with a huge, glaring neon sign that blinked "GIRLS GIRLS GIRLS." A few hookers loitered in front of the bar, but Rocky didn't recognize any of them. They all seemed young, too young. He almost heaved a sigh of relief when he passed Andy's Italian-American Bar. Not everything had changed.

Suddenly remembering that it was Paulie's birthday, he headed home.

As he sped through the streets he kept wondering how he had forgotten his promise to Adrian. She was the last person in the world he wanted to disappoint. Before he knew it, he was in his neighborhood.

This area had changed, too. When he had first moved in it was a quiet, upper-middle-class residential section. But Rocky's arrival had signaled the beginning of a new affluence for the neighborhood. It became chic to live there. Real estate prices soared and privacy diminished as people flocked to see where the champ lived. It became so bad that Rocky had to build a six-foot-high brick wall around his property to insure some peace and quiet.

He pulled up to the gate that blocked the driveway, took the electronic beeper from the glove compartment, and pushed the button. The gate opened like the arm of a silent sentry waving Rocky in. Rocky entered and the gate closed behind him. He parked the car in front of the garage and got out. Piles of boards, rolls of insulation, electrical pipes, and other building materials littered the area. Rocky wearily eyed them and the scaffolding at the end of the garage. What had started out to be a minor expansion of the house somehow had mushroomed into a never-ending project. He would be glad when the hammering and sawing stopped.

He walked toward the front door, but before he reached it, Rocky Junior zoomed out, a bright orange party hat on his head and the camera in his hands. The blinding light of the sun gun was aimed directly at Rocky's face, and his hand shielded his eyes in protest. Rocky Junior continued to film away, oblivious to his father's discomfort.

"Dad, you're late!" the boy exclaimed. "Mommy's gonna yell at you!"

The dramatic statement, coupled with the sight of his son dancing around with the camera, made Rocky laugh. Maybe his boy was going to end up in the movies.

"So how're you doing?" Rocky was beginning to do some fancy footwork of his own as he tried to avoid the glaring light.

"Fine. If you don't hurry, you're gonna get it. This is a warning!"

The boy moved in for a close-up.

Rocky danced back, bobbing and weaving as if he were in the ring. Rocky Junior plowed after him, a formidable pint-size opponent. They were a whirling circle of light in the black night.

"You know, we're kinda bright out here. Maybe we're disturbing Mother Nature, don't you think?"

"A little, Dad," his son agreed. Then, in more ominous tones, he added, "Dad, I wouldn't wanna be you. You

13

better hurry or else!" The boy momentarily stopped filming and inspected his father more closely. "Where'd you get the hat?"

"A friend gave it to me."

"Who punched you in the eye, Daddy?"

"Same friend."

Rocky opened the trunk of the car and removed a small box with an even smaller wrapped present on it.

"That's weird," Rocky Junior said, resuming filming.

With a split-second move Rocky jumped forward and put his hand over the sun gun light. Rocky Junior's face crumbled in disappointment.

"Okay, keep on filming, but get in back of me."

The boy's face lit up as he hurried around his father. Rocky walked toward the front door.

"Better hurry, Dad."

Rocky quickened his pace. "Y'know, you're getting a very loud personality."

"Don't go too fast or you go out of focus."

As he opened the door Rocky laughed at his son's contradictory commands. Maybe his son was military material—hurry up, slow down.

Paulie sat at the living room table, a despondent look on his face and the party hat clamped onto his head by a taut rubber band that vanished in the folds of his double chin. A transistor radio sat on the table blaring the results of a ball game, but Paulie wasn't listening. He didn't even know who was playing, much less the score. Several colorful pieces of crepe paper stretched across the room along with a sagging "Happy Birthday" sign. Party favors decorated the table, but Paulie didn't pay any attention to them. He had thought that the party would be over by now and he'd be cruising the streets in his new car. In his mind he could see it clearly. The car looked exactly like Rocky's, only it was flaming red. The older he got, the more honest he got. He wanted all the attention he could get. He might even drive down South Street and see the old gang. Show them how Paulie's been moving up in the world. Somebody had told him that Adrian's old store had been turned into a real classy bar. That might be just the place to test his new car's effectiveness on the opposite sex.

Paulie heard laughter, then Rocky entered the living room empty-handed. Rocky Junior trailed after him, still filming away like mad. When Rocky saw Paulie he laughed even louder. The party hat made Paulie look like a cross between a grizzly bear and a clown.

"Yo! It's about time!"

"Sorry, Paulie." Rocky shrugged, trying to stifle his laughter.

In the kitchen Adrian heard the commotion and started lighting the candles with long fireplace matches. She still had to be careful about singeing her wrists. She hoped the candles were dripless as the package promised.

Rocky fought his laughter into a smile, but then Rocky Junior with the eye of a true cameraman, turned his bright light on Paulie. Paulie squirmed like someone under attack. Rocky broke into laughter again.

"Hey, what's so funny?" Paulie asked. "Let me in on the joke."

"It's nothing. Nothing at all."

Paulie looked dubious. Nobody was going to put anything over on him, especially on his birthday. But then it occurred to Paulie that nobody gave presents to someone for being surly. Besides, he thought as he watched his nephew bobbing and weaving with the almost-too-heavy camera in his hands, Rocky was laughing at the boy, not at him. Paulie began laughing, too. Rocky Junior did look pretty comical.

Adrian stepped out of the kitchen, walked over to Rocky, and hugged and kissed him.

"I'm sorry, Ad—"

But Adrian interrupted him. "Oh, Rocky, it's just great that you're here." She glanced pointedly at Paulie. "Now you can stop calling him names."

Rocky patted his son's head. "She yells real nice, huh, kid?"

Rocky Junior nodded, a big smile on his face.

"If we waited much longer it would be time for my next birthday," Paulie stated impatiently.

Adrian ignored Paulie and asked Rocky, "Where were you?"

"Getting punched." Rocky took the movie camera from a disappointed Rocky Junior. "Let me do this." He started playing with the camera, filming the party.

15

"No, seriously," Adrian persisted.

"Seriously."

Looking at the redness around his eye Adrian knew there was more to the story, but she also knew Rocky well enough to wait until he wanted to tell her.

"So why don't we get the cake in here and get this celebration going?" Paulie felt it was time that someone got the party back on the right track. First the cake, then the present. Simple as one, two, three—then, *va-va-voom*, he was off to South Street and who knew what.

Rocky Junior chimed in, "You're gonna love your present, Uncle Paulie."

"So where is it?" Paulie asked, hoping the impatience didn't echo in his voice.

Adrian went to the kitchen door and held it open while Rocky Junior blew a party horn, making a *ta-ta-ta* sound. Rocky moved in close to catch Paulie's expression.

Paulie wondered how a car was going to fit through the door.

A robot walked through the door. It was about five feet tall and rolled on wheels. In its outstretched arms it held the flaming birthday cake. A perpetual "Have a nice day" smile was painted around the microphone box on its face. A pink ribbon was tied decoratively around its square head.

Paulie stared at it, speechless, then asked, "What the hell's that?"

"Your present," Rocky Junior said proudly.

Paulie stared at the robot, then at the cake, then back at the robot, a horrified expression on his face. He realized that forty wasn't going to be the big turning point that he had expected. There wasn't going to be any sports car to help him along. Forty years old and a robot owner— who would have believed it?

"Yo," he blurted out, "I wanted a sports car for my birthday." But then, remembering that all this was being immortalized by the movie camera, he attempted a feeble laugh. "Not a walking trash can! This is extremely psycho."

Paulie closed his eyes, but when he opened them the robot was still there holding the cake.

"I don't believe this. . . ."

"Since you don't have any friends, we thought you'd

16

like it," Adrian said, beginning to be embarrassed at her brother's reaction. You aren't supposed to look a gift robot in the mouth, she thought.

Rocky continued to move around with the camera, turning from Paulie to the robot, back to Paulie, swinging over to Adrian. It was very easy to see where Rocky Junior had gotten his moves. He went in for a tight close-up of Paulie's tortured smile.

"It'll keep you company. C'mon, pretend you're happy," Rocky advised.

Paulie's smile tightened as he stared incredulously at the robot.

"Yeah, c'mon." Rocky Junior playfully slapped Paulie's shoulder. What could be wrong with his uncle? The robot was the most wonderful present in the whole world. Adults . . . they sure acted strange sometimes. He noticed a can of Redi-whip on the table and picked it up for closer inspection.

"Please make a wish," the robot said in a monotone.

"What? It talks! This thing is creepy," Paulie said.

Adrian and Rocky were too busy laughing to feel sympathy for Paulie.

"Please make a wish. Time is money," the robot continued.

"Relax, metal head" Paulie commanded, feeling that it was time for him to get a better grip on the situation. "I'd like to make a wish. I wish I wasn't having this nightmare."

Rocky Junior laughed. He was Paulie's best audience.

"Wanna help me put out this forest fire on the count of three?"

The boy dutifully nodded his head.

"One—two—three!"

Paulie leaned forward, blowing on the candles, but Rocky Junior turned the can of Redi-whip on the cake and sprayed the candles out with a blast of cream. Paulie was dumbfounded. What kind of party was this? First a robot, now his nephew acting a little peculiar. Jeez . . .

"They're out," Rocky Junior announced.

Paulie glanced at Rocky. "You're gonna have gruesome problems with this kid."

Rocky focused on the cake as Adrian sliced it.

"Please make a wish," the robot repeated.

Paulie was wondering as he took his piece of cake how much of a trade-in he'd get for the robot on a sports car.

It was late. Aside from a lamp in the far corner of the study, the only illumination was the glow from the monitor screen of Rocky's home computer. But there was enough light to see the dark mahogany desk, rows of bookshelves lining the east wall, and paintings hung randomly. It was too dark to verify it, but the paintings were originals— expensive ones.

Rocky sat at the computer working on an English program he had inserted in the disk drive. Questions would appear on the monitor screen and Rocky would type in the answers. Sometimes the answers would be a simple yes or no; other times he would have to diagram sentences, complete phrases, or correct spelling. It was hard work for Rocky, but he gamely persisted at it. A correct answer got a *bonk*; an incorrect answer got a *boing*. Rocky hated the *boings*. Another question flashed across the screen. Rocky typed in his answer. *Boing*. That's it, I should've quit when I was ahead, Rocky decided, yawning and rubbing his eyes.

The door opened slightly and Adrian stuck her head in.

"I'm going to bed. Is there anything I can get you first?"

"No, thank you. I'll be there in a second myself," he answered, smiling.

Adrian withdrew and closed the door.

Rocky got up from the computer and went to the desk. He opened one of the side drawers and took out the box and package. He smiled to himself.

Rocky closely inspected his eye in the mirror. The harsh bathroom light made it look worse than it was. Oh, well, the bedroom lights were dimmer. It wouldn't be as noticeable. Aside from the eye, he didn't look too bad, but his hair didn't satisfy him. He sloshed some hair tonic in his hands, then ran them through his hair. Next, a few quick swipes with his comb. Better. Feel good, look good, smell good. He applied cologne to his face and chest. He pulled at the elastic of his pajama bottoms and splashed on a few more drops. Perfect. He opened the box and took out a cake. He balanced the cake in his right hand

and picked up the package with his left.

The bedside lamp bathed Adrian's face in a warm glow. She turned the page of the book she was reading. It wasn't any more interesting than the previous page. She closed the book and yawned. She wished Rocky would hurry.

As if on cue, Rocky exited the bathroom, hands full.

"Rocky?" she asked, smiling quizzically.

"You noticed."

"Why do you have that cake?"

"'Cause the party's not over. It's a special night."

"It's Wednesday," she said, humoring him.

"Yeah, it's definitely Wednesday and it's almost nine years that you've been married to me. Impossible, but you done it. So here's the prize."

"But our anniversary's a week away."

"Why wait?"

She got out of bed, took the cake from his hand, and inspected it carefully. On top of the cake were two figures, bride and groom; both were in boxing stances and wearing gloves. Adrian laughed.

"Has it been that rough?" she asked.

"It's been excellent. Open your present."

Adrian put the cake on the bedside table. Rocky gave her the wrapped package. She opened it and pulled out a set of pearls. They looked luminescent in the lamplight. Adrian stared at them, her eyes appreciating their delicate beauty.

"Like it?"

She kissed him. "They're beautiful."

"It's incredible that those things reside in an oyster, y'know," Rocky said knowingly. Not all his time at the computer had been spent getting *boings*.

"They're so beautiful. Thank you, honey."

Rocky put his hands on Adrian's shoulders. He never ceased to be amazed by how fragile she felt. It brought back his old "bull in a china shop" feeling. But experience had taught him that in many ways she was as strong as he was. He had learned that on a windswept California beach. She just had a deceptive outward appearance. A beautiful, deceptive outward appearance. His right hand went up to her head and touched her hair. It was incredibly soft. He brushed some strands back from her forehead just to have an excuse for his hand to linger there.

19

"You're more beautiful," he said.

"So are you."

His arms slid over her shoulders, pulling her closer to him. She felt warm and pliant. He knew her body as well as he did his own, but he was continually surprised by the sensations he felt when she pressed against him. He had been no virgin when he met her, but nobody had ever made him feel the way she did. She had taught him tenderness with the touch of her hands and the look in her eyes. It had changed him, enlarged his world. Now he couldn't do without it.

"Y'know, what's amazing is that after all these years everything still feels new."

"Think it'll ever change between us?" she asked, her head leaning against his chest, her arms encircling his muscular bulk. How could she ever have gotten this lucky? She marveled every time she touched him. It was hard to remember that she had once taken for granted that she would end up an old maid—unloved, unwanted.

"Absolutely no way."

"I hope not."

He pulled back a little so he could look into her eyes.

"Remember, I told you the night we got married that you're never getting rid of me...."

Adrian nodded, smiling at the memory.

"Well, you're not."

They pressed against each other again and kissed gently. Her arms went around his neck as the kiss continued and intensified. They were so close, they seemed like one body.

Paulie walked unsteadily down the hallway, a beer can sloshing in his hand. The robot trailed after him like a dog. What a night, Paulie thought. No car, a tin can monster, a foamy birthday cake. Why me, he wondered, why is it always me? He could hear the wheels of the robot gliding across the carpet. He scowled and faced his tracker.

"Quit following me, you moving junkyard," Paulie growled.

The robot stopped, waiting for Paulie.

Muttering, Paulie continued down the hallway. When he reached his room, the robot was right behind him.

"Listen, I'm warning you!"

20

"I will wake you up," the robot intoned. "What time do you wish to get up? Pick a time, please. I can be programmed to make coffee, tea, warm milk, or hot cocoa. How many cups, please? Please program the number of cups. Please program your wake up call. Time is money."

Paulie crushed the beer can in front of the robot's face but got no response. He figured the robot was smart enough to know it was just an aluminum can. Disgusted, he went into his bedroom, slamming the door behind him.

The robot bumped uncomprehendingly against the door a few times, then stopped and became a silent sentinel.

A few seconds later the door opened and Paulie stuck his head out.

"Hey, battery brain, you want a nice, healthy relationship? Then just shut up and c'mon in."

The robot dutifully rolled into the bedroom.

Before the door closed, Paulie's voice could be heard in the darkness of the bedroom: "Listen, wake me up at ten and bring me a cold beer...."

# Chapter 2

The 747 Air France jet cut through the clear morning air. Even though it was going at a tremendous speed, from a distance you could track it with a slow-moving finger. In the cockpit the impression of stillness was reinforced. There was no turbulent roar of engines or screeching of wind. Everything was silent—even the crew members, except for an occassional cough or body movement. They were nearing the end of the Paris–New York flight and they were tired.

The captain, a solid, responsible-looking man with his thoughts on retirement, picked up the microphone and announced in French, "In fifteen minutes we will be landing at Kennedy International Airport in the Borough of Queens in the City of New York in the State of New York. Our landing time will be 10:15 A.M. Be sure to set your watches. The temperature in New York is a balmy eighty degrees. Observe the "No Smoking" sign and keep your seat belts on until we have come to a complete stop. Upon deplaning you will enter the International Arrivals Building, where you will be processed through U.S. Customs. Enjoy your stay in New York City and thank you for flying Air France."

He repeated the message in English, German, and Spanish. He hung up the microphone and steepened his descent. He could see New York below. His body ached;

he was getting too old to do this much longer. Maybe he'd put in his resignation next month. He owed that to his passengers and crew. If he wasn't at his best, he shouldn't be flying. But if he didn't fly, what would he do? He laughed at himself. Walk. If you didn't fly, you walked.

Michelle, the stewardess for the first-class section, fastened her seat belt and glanced out the window. From the air, New York looked exactly like what it was: three islands connected by bridges to one another and to the mainland. She had a twenty-four hour layover in New York before her turnaround and she was looking forward to it. New York was a party town and she was a party girl. It would help make up for the flight, which had been boring. The whole plane had been reserved by Russians. They had deplaned from an Aeroflot flight at Orly and boarded the Air France jet. Aeroflot flights had been barred from the U.S. after the Russian invasion of Afghanistan. Michelle wasn't up on her politics and she didn't care about Afghanistan or boycotts. She was more interested in getting out of her uniform and into some sheets, preferably not alone.

Five passengers were in the first-class section: Ivan Drago, his wife Ludmilla, Nicolai Koloff, Igor Rimsky, and Manuel Vega. Michelle found Drago the most interesting of the five. He was immense, with a body that threatened to burst out of his suit. He was handsome, but in a cold way. His face was composed of hard, angular planes and displayed even less emotion than his steely gray eyes. Yet she could imagine his blond hair glistening like gold in the sunlight. Attractive but dangerous, a combination that Michelle had pursued before with mixed results. His wife, Ludmilla, approached six feet in height and also had a muscular, athletic body. She smiled occasionally, but it was all teeth and no eyes. Michelle thought they could be nominees for robot couple of the year.

Igor Rimsky looked uncomfortable in his suit. He was short and squat, but with a powerful barrel chest that gave him a gruff but commanding presence. A prototype for the Russian Bear. He was Drago's coach.

One look at Nicolai Koloff was enough for Michelle to decide that he was a diplomatic attaché. The briefcase, the expensive suit and shoes, the hard eyes and quick smile all added up to a politician. Politicians looked the same no matter what country they came from. They even seemed to use the same cologne, scented but unidentifiable.

The Cuban, Manuel Vega, appeared the most accessible of the five. He looked like a man used to hard work and long hours, a survivor of revolutions and regimes. He sat apart from the Russians and was the only one who had openly admired Michelle's obvious assets. Unfortunately, his face bore the scars of too many years in the boxing profession. Michelle found him pug ugly yet cute. He was Drago's trainer.

Talk during the flight had been limited to a few whispered conversations in Russian and perfunctory refusals of food and beverages. They were polite but cold. Michelle would have preferred a wandering hand up the back of her skirt—anything to break the monotony. Everybody seemed too damned reserved. It was obvious that they weren't going to New York as casual tourists. At least it was nearly over.

The plane jolted slightly as the wheels hit the runway. The engines and brakes could be heard as the plane slowed and skidded to a stop.

Michelle unfastened her seat belt and put on her best smile. It was a dazzler.

It was bedlam inside the International Arrivals Building. Policemen dressed in blue were stationed at intervals in the corridor that led from the boarding gate. They tried hard to scan the crowd with piercing eyes, but the excitement generated by the roving bands of reporters with their entourage of Minicam operators was too much. The police were part of the crowd they were trying to control. Plainclothes detectives with white plastic earphones moved through the crowd, eyes searching for potential trouble. Occassionally one would mutter into a palm-sized microphone. They blended into the crowd like the moon into a dark night.

All in all, it was a festive affair. For weeks the press and other media had been preparing the American public for Ivan Drago, the Russian super heavyweight champion, and people had turned out on cue like paid pickets. They were all ages, sizes, shapes, and colors—the curious, the bored, the unemployed, the dilettantes. Some carried signs bearing anti-Russian sentiments, but most were just curious. When news of the plane's landing was announced the anticipation level became almost tangible. A few people in the crowd even started chanting: "The Russians are coming, the Russians are coming." But the boarding gate remained empty. The crowd continued to push and sway back and forth like wheat in the wind.

When the plane had come to a complete stop Koloff motioned to the security agents in the second-class compartment, and they responded as one by lining the sides of the jetway. The four remaining passengers fell into position behind Koloff. Drago gripped his wife's hand and for a moment there was a hint of emotion in his eyes, but it passed quickly, unnoticed by all except Ludmilla. She understood his apprehension. They were strangers in a strange land.

Koloff and his entourage started walking down the jetway. Their footsteps echoed hollowly. They proceeded in step like a military procession. Everyone looked straight ahead, expressionless. They were ready for America.

When they walked through the landing gate reporters nearly swarmed all over them, but they were effectively shielded by American and Russian security men. The onlooking crowd was awed into silence by their first glance at Drago. He was so large that he towered over the security people protecting him. The crowd muttered comments of disbelief. They had been expecting somebody unusual, but not this unusual. Drago glared at them, mistaking their amazement for hostility. The head of American security told Koloff that customs had been taken care of and that limousines were waiting outside to take them to the Russian United Nations Mission on East Sixty-seventh Street. Koloff nodded and started moving brusquely forward. It was a phalanx maneuver that the ancient Romans would have been proud of. They moved through the crowd with the force and certainty of a knife.

But the reporters were adamant. They earned their living talking to people who didn't want to talk. It was a game that they knew well and enjoyed.

"Would you answer a few questions?" a reporter queried, shoving a microphone into Koloff's face.

"Yes, later," Koloff answered, straining to be as polite as possible. This would never be allowed in Moscow, he thought to himself.

Another reporter managed to squeeze close to Drago. "When are you going to fight, Drago?"

Koloff hurriedly stepped between Drago and the reporter.

"We talk later, please," Koloff insisted, his smile becoming tighter. How were these reporters managing to get so close? It was like trying to hold back water with your hands. They were everywhere. And they were drips. Koloff prided himself on being able to make jokes in colloquial English. Unfortunately, he couldn't share this one with anyone else. Later he would tell it and retell it. Koloff didn't know it, but he was infamous in the diplomatic corps for this failing.

"How long are you here for?" another reporter asked.

"As long as necessary."

"Necessary to do exactly what?" the reporter persisted.

"We talk at press conference." Koloff's voice was beginning to take on a certain gruffness.

"Is it definite that the Soviet Union will enter professional boxing?"

Koloff pushed the microphone away from his face. "Please. No more talk now. We will talk at press conference. Excuse us."

The security men tightened up and the cordon managed to push through the crowd, out of the building, and into the waiting limousines.

Once inside the limousines, everyone relaxed. It had been awkward, but not as bad as they had expected.

The limousines took off. The Russians had landed.

# Chapter 3

Cora Creed gazed out through the sliding glass doors of her living room and watched her husband Apollo swing lazily in the backyard hammock, a drink clutched carelessly in his hand. Her fine-featured face was calm and untroubled, but her eyes shone with the intensity of deep thought. She was trying to figure out what Apollo was thinking. The fact that she wasn't having much success didn't bother her. She had been married to him for seventeen years but sometimes she felt as if she had just met him. At first glance they seemed an unlikely couple—the attraction of opposites. She was quiet and reserved, preferring to keep a low profile and stay out of the public view. Apollo, on the other hand, seemed to draw energy from constant exposure to the public. Attention was a necessity to him. He basked in publicity while she required privacy. But it was a successful relationship. They had stayed together through the good and bad times, each fulfilling some secret need in the other. Cora was pondering whether they were on the verge of a good time or about to enter a bad time.

When Rocky had defeated Apollo in the rematch, she had almost been relieved. All those years of worrying about her husband being injured in the ring seemed over. But then she realized that injuries didn't have to be physical. In fact, Apollo appeared more vulnerable to psychic jabs than he ever was to tangible roundhouses. His ego didn't control his life, but it certainly was an important influence.

The years since he had lost the championship had been trying, but Apollo had managed to stay close to the action by working as a sports commentator and appearing on various talk shows. It wasn't the same as being the champ, but it was something. It kept him from sinking into anonymity. But it began to get very mechanical, just a series of safe jobs, and Apollo needed risks. Then he had concocted the idea of managing Rocky for a rematch with Clubber Lang. It was like a blood transfusion. It had been a rebirth for him as well as for Rocky. He had been revitalized by being part of the show again instead of just commenting on it. Now that was over, and Cora was worried.

Apollo had told her about the secret match with Rocky. Too many years had passed for Apollo still to be bothered by one second of history. It was time for him to find new goals that could harness his energy. Rocky and Apollo, Cora mused to herself, were two of a kind. Unchangeables in a constantly changing world. She was glad that they were friends. When time had stripped them of their titles and abilities they would still have the friendship. In a way, she felt sorry for them. They, and others like them, were destined to become anachronisms. For them boxing was more than just a sport that led to fame and riches. They weren't contract players with calculating machines and tax shelters for hearts. Boxing was part of them. It was that simple.

She chided herself for being overly dramatic. Apollo was a mature adult. She was his wife, not his guardian. He'd find a way to end his current restlessness. He always had. She was the one that was overreacting, not him.

Cora went into the kitchen and took some fish out of the freezer. She was glad that today was the maid's day off. There were times when *she* needed something to do, too.

The rocking of the hammock was putting Apollo to sleep. He barely felt the glass as it slipped from his hand.

It landed in the grass with a dull thud that snapped him out of his dreams. Luckily the tumbler was plastic, being part of the set from the poolside bar, and it didn't shatter. Apollo opened his eyes, picked up the glass, and drained its contents. He felt groggy. That was his third drink of the afternoon. He stared up at the blue sky sprinkled with puffy white clouds that looked like floating mountains. A jet streaked across the sky, then disappeared before the noise of its flight reached Apollo's ears. He sat up in the hammock and rubbed his face. Bleary, he thought, that's what I am, bleary. On a beautiful day like this it was criminal to be getting smashed. I've got to straighten up my act, he thought.

A portable television sat on a nearby lawn table. Apollo yawned, got up, and turned the set on. A small point of color began in the middle of the screen and spread like a cancer until a local news anchorwoman was discernible. Apollo checked his watch with surprise. He had lost more of the afternoon than he had thought.

The newswoman finished up a story on a local fire that had killed three people and injured two more. Arson was suspected, she reported brightly. When they returned from a commercial break the sports would be next.

Apollo sat back on the hammock and waited. She hadn't lied. Soon the face of a chubby sportscaster with a too-tight tie that gave him a choked look filled the screen. After exchanging a few fire and sports jokes with the anchorwoman he turned and looked directly into the camera, eyes twinkling, voice professionally virile and monotonous.

"Well, today may have proved to be a landmark in sports," he began. "After unraveling years' worth of red tape, Russia will now throw its hat in the ring—the prize ring, that is."

Apollo's eyes were suddenly intent on the screen. He leaned forward and turned up the volume. Another jet streaked across the sky, but Apollo was oblivious to it.

"Today the American public met Ivan Drago, the Russian boxing superstar. The introductions were made by his wife, Ludmilla Vobet, a double Olympic gold medalist in swimming."

The sportscaster dissolved from the screen to be

replaced by a tape of a full-blown press conference. Seated behind a table swamped by microphones were Ivan Drago with Ludmilla directly by his side, Igor Rimsky next to her, and Nicolai Koloff flanking Drago on the other side. The glaring camera lights gave a strobelike effect to the proceedings. The reporters were seated in chairs facing the table. They appeared momentarily subdued as they waited for a signal from the table to begin the conference.

Ludmilla nervously shuffled some papers in front of her.

The last of the camera crews settled into place.

The only noise now was the occasional creak of a chair or a muffled cough.

"Today the Soviet Union has officially entered professional boxing," Ludmilla began reading from her prepared speech. "My husband, the great, undefeated world amateur heavyweight champion, Ivan Drago, has come with his trainers to America to compete as an international sportsman and goodwill ambassador." Her voice became more relaxed and natural as she continued reading. "My husband is a dedicated athlete and father and will be the first to compete. It is wonderful to be in your country, and we hope other athletes from our country will follow." She ended the speech with a brilliant smile.

The reporters, having done their duty by listening courteously to the speech, were on their feet and firing a barrage of questions.

One reporter managed to yell loud enough to be heard by the panel. "Drago! Who will be your first fight?"

Koloff nodded at Ludmilla.

"My husband does not speak English very well, but he would like to compete against anyone who is qualified."

The questions started coming again, so fast that Ludmilla wondered if anyone was even listening to her answers.

"Has Drago ever boxed against a real professional?"

Drago's comprehension of English seemed to be good enough for him to understand the content of this question. He glared at the reporter who had asked it. Ludmilla put her hand over his. A tight smile broke over his face.

"Not yet," she answered. "But having been trained in

Russia and in Cuba by the great boxing coach, Manuel Vega, and now by Igor Rimsky, we hope he is qualified to do so."

"Hope?"

"Well, I don't want to sound too confident," Ludmilla said, coating her words with sugar.

Some of the newsmen smiled cynically at each other. They had attended too many of these affairs to let a novice like Ludmilla lead them around by the nose. She was charming, but she was full of crap.

Koloff, sensing a shift from Ludmilla was needed, jumped into the conference.

"If possible, we wish first to have a friendly exhibition bout with your famous champion, Rocky Balboa, as a way to introduce Drago to America."

"Has Balboa responded?"

"No," Koloff admitted, "he has not responded." More noise, shuffling of feet, voices overriding one another.

"Drago is still an amateur. What makes you think he could stand the pressure of fighting someone as seasoned and strong as Balboa?"

Drago's countenance darkened considerably. Koloff quickly nodded at Rimsky to answer.

"Drago is the most perfect athlete in the world. There is no one who can match his strength, his endurance, or his aggressiveness."

"You make it sound like he's indestructible," the reporter continued.

"Yes," Rimsky said simply, "he is."

Amid a hubbub of noise from the reporters the press conference faded from the screen to be replaced by the chuckling visage of the sportscaster.

"No shortage of confidence there," he chortled; then, in a more serious vein, he added, "Can this mammoth, Cuban-trained Russian who's already been nicknamed 'the Siberian Express' wreak havoc in the professional heavy-weight ranks? Time will tell, but one thing is certain— his first fight will be one hot ticket.... We'll be right back with an update on today's professional football score-board."

Apollo switched the television off.

The ghost of a smile played on his lips and his eyes

31

tightened as he stared unseeingly into the distance. If a brain at work made noise, Apollo's would have sounded like an auto factory going full blast. For the first time in days, he felt ravenously hungry. He started towards the house. He had to feed that brain because it was going to be working overtime.

# Chapter 4

Rocky's study was littered with toys. Star Wars characters rested in large plastic trucks. A Big Wheel tricycle missing one pedal was parked in front of the desk. Puzzle pieces were scattered on the carpet in a manner that assured that the puzzle would never be completed—the first of many mysteries in a young boy's life. A neglected teddy bear missing one arm slept peacefully by the bookshelves, glad that his term of service was over. Periodically the housekeeper would clean up the study, but inevitable Rocky Junior would drag the toys back one at a time. He needed something to distract him while he watched his dad work.

But today Rocky Junior was the one sitting at the computer, not his dad. He wasn't too pleased with the situation. The green glow of the monitor screen gave off the same ominous vibrations as his teacher in preschool.

Paulie stood in the doorway with a beer can in his hand and an amused smile on his face. His now-constant companion, the robot, waited a respectful distance behind him. Paulie shared his nephew's opinion of computers. It never occurred to him that his new-found friend was nothing more than an elaborate computer.

Rocky Junior squirmed in the chair and glanced wistfully at the stationary Big Wheel. Even with one pedal missing he could make it speed down the hallways fast enough to be a menace. That was fun. This was work.

Rocky stood behind his son, literally looking over his shoulder.

"Okay, now hit the return key," Rocky urged.

His son dutifully tapped the return key with his finger and another question unfolded on the monitor screen. Rocky Junior stared intently at the screen, moving his mouth as he read the words there.

*Who was the thirty-fifth—*

The next word was too long. Rocky Junior could make out the individual letters but couldn't put them together as a single word. He looked to his father for help.

"Sound it out."

"Pres ... presi..."

"President," Paulie guessed as he moved closer to the computer.

*Who was the thirty-fifth president of the United States?*

Rocky Junior kept staring at the question. He didn't know what number the current president was, much less who was the thirty-fifth. This was exactly like school except there weren't any recesses.

"Why can't I go hit the punching bag?"

"C'mon, you gotta learn this stuff," Rocky insisted. "Now, who was the thirty-fifth president?"

"Why do I have to know that? I wanna hit the bag."

Paulie was having a *sotto voce* conference with the robot as he tried to find out the answer.

Rocky understood his son's frustration; he had felt it many times himself as he sat in front of the computer. But like every father he wanted his son to be better than himself and he felt that the computer could be an invaluable tool in achieving that goal. Rocky Junior wasn't a slum kid who had to spend his time concentrating on survival instead of going to school. He had a plethora of advantages, and Rocky was determined to see that he made good use of them.

"Forget the bag," Rocky said, patting his son's head. "Everybody's got gaps in the brain and it's important to fill those gaps with facts and data when you're young, 'cause you're gonna need it when you're older."

Rocky Junior wasn't sure that his question had been

34

adequately answered, but the determined look on his father's face made him turn back to the computer. His brow furrowed in concentration. If his father said it was important, it was important.

Paulie turned down the volume control as the robot answered his question.

"So what's the answer?" Rocky persisted.

"Who's the last president to be killed?" Paulie chimed in, never wanting to miss an opportunity to sound smarter than he looked.

Rocky scowled at Paulie. He thought there were better ways to remember the thirty-fifth president.

The boy said hesitantly, "John F. Kennedy. Is that right?"

"Yeah, absolutely. Now punch it in the computer and remember two n's in Kennedy."

Rocky Junior slowly typed in the answer and was rewarded with a *bonk*. A big smile spread across his face. Maybe computers weren't that bad after all.

Paulie took a huge swig from his beer can and burped. "My philosophy says he should be learning how to fight."

"Why?" Rocky asked. It never ceased to amaze him how the biggest proponents of physical conflicts were people who were never going to be involved in one. When he was in the ring he had looked out at the audience and seen blood lust in the eyes of people who had never been hit in their lives. He didn't know whether it was cowardice or common sense, but they had no conception of what fighting actually was. It hurt. It hurt like hell. They wouldn't be able to take it. Paulie was no exception. He wouldn't last a minute in a prize ring. Rocky didn't hold this against Paulie. It just made him wonder why he wanted to encourage a small kid to fight.

"Why?" Rocky repeated.

"'Cause punks are gonna squash his head. He's the champ's kid, okay? How's that for facts and data?" Paulie asserted. He put his hand on Rocky Junior's small shoulder. "You want an intensely squashed head?"

Rocky Junior shook his head, still smiling. His uncle was nice, but he sure said some strange things. It was getting hard to tell whether he was being funny or serious.

"Nicely put, Paulie," Rocky sighed. There were times when he wished that Adrian had been an only child.

"Thanks," Paulie said, congratulating himself on having made an intelligent point. He could figure things out for himself; he didn't need a computer when he had common sense.

"Beer, dear."

The computer rolled forward and offered Paulie a fresh beer. Paulie squashed his old can and deposited it in the litterbag that had been tied around the robot's waist like an apron. It landed with a dull *clunk* as it hit the empties that were already there.

Paulie popped open his new beer and took a swallow. It was a good life.

The gate to Rocky's house swung open and Apollo Creed drove his car in and down the driveway, parking by a pair of stone lions that flanked the sidewalk leading to the front door. He momentarily viewed the construction litter with curiosity. He had been caught in that trap before. You asked for a simple thing like an extra door. Everybody smiles and says there's no problem. A month later half the house is torn up and everybody is smiling but you.

His mind went back to the reason for his visit. He had been excited ever since he had watched the newscast. Cora had noticed it the moment he had entered the house. She had questioned him about it, but he truthfully had no answers then, just a feeling that emanated from his guts and would eventually work its way up to his brain. A few days later he had it, or was close to having it, but first he had to talk to Rocky. Rocky was the linchpin in the plan. Without him there was nothing to talk about.

Apollo got out of the car and started up the sidewalk.

Rocky Junior was still seated in front of the computer, but now a sports quiz had been inserted in the disk drive. This one was fun. It became a contest to see who could answer the questions first. Rocky was in the lead, Rocky Junior was second, and a grumbling Paulie was last. They had made him send his robot out of the room. He was still complaining that that was unfair. He and the robot

36

were legitimate partners. Besides, his beer was running low.

The intercom buzzed.

Rocky pushed the speak button, said "Yeah," then released it.

Adrian's voice sounded tinny as she said, "Rocky, Apollo's here."

"What? You're kidding!"

"No, Rock. It's the Master of Disaster in the flesh." Even Apollo's voice sounded strange filtered through the intercom.

"I'll be right down."

Rocky Junior looked pensively at his father. "Not another rematch, I hope."

"No, no more. Listen, keep studying. Put the history disk back in, okay?"

Rocky Junior nodded his head.

"And Paulie, let him work. Got it?"

"Got it," Paulie said in his most sincere manner.

Rocky left the room, curious about Apollo's visit.

Paulie switched off the computer. The green light faded and then vanished. A push of the button on the remote control device brought the robot back with a fresh beer. Paulie pulled a deck of cards out of his shirt pocket.

"You still have that jar full of pennies?"

"Yes, but—"

"Remember how to play gin?"

"Kind of," Rocky Junior answered.

"Let's go to your room."

Paulie riffled the cards as they left the study.

Apollo was in the living room, sitting on the couch. He was dressed in a snappy business suit complete with a muted striped tie. He rose from the couch, hand extended, when Rocky entered the room. Rocky shook hands, his eyes appreciating the suit. It was obvious that this was more than a social visit. He was curious about what Apollo was up to. He was always up to something. That was one of his endearing qualities.

"Hey, Stallion, what've you been doing?"

"Nothing much."

The housekeeper came into the room and asked if they

37

wanted drinks. They both declined.

"Nice suit," Rocky ventured.

"Clothes make the man."

Rocky knew that Apollo knew that he was curious, but Apollo was playing him along like a fish. Rocky also knew that Apollo played this game a lot better than he did, so he decided to end it.

"Why're you here?"

"I like that," Apollo said, smiling. "Direct. Right to the point."

"Which we still haven't gotten to," Rocky reminded him.

Apollo's smile got bigger. "Have you been keeping up with the news?"

Rocky watched the television reports and skimmed through the paper, but he wasn't a news addict. No recent event that might have prompted this visit came to mind.

"Not much, why?"

Apollo's smile faded, but his eyes still gleamed.

"Let's step outside."

Rocky shrugged and nodded his head. He'd play it Apollo's way.

Rocky noticed the vintage, exotic Rolls parked in the driveway.

"Thought you'd be driving something newer by now, just for a change."

"There's a lot of things I don't want to change. And at least when I raise the hood of this baby I can see things that look familiar. Sparks plugs, distributor cap, water pump, y'know what I mean. These new cars are all modern technology," Apollo said scornfully. "Bust down on the road and you're trying to fix a computer, not a car. You can't even get at anything without jerking the engine. Everything's getting too fancy, too complicated."

"Could be," Rocky agreed. "But that's the way things are going. Progress."

"I ain't against progress, but we gotta keep the basics. There are some things that just gotta be protected."

"What are you getting at?" Rocky asked, sitting down on one of the stone lions.

"You heard about the Russians, right?"

"Yeah, they live in Russia."

"You know what I mean. The ones that just came over here. The boxer," Apollo said his voice showing a trace of frustration.

"Yeah, I know. Saw 'em on TV." Rocky enjoyed turning the tables on Apollo and watching him get exasperated.

"The Russians are serious about this giant taking your title, you know that?"

"I heard some talk."

"It's more than talk." Apollo's voice was serious now. "Have they gotten to you yet?"

"They asked the Commission to let us fight an exhibition bout."

"So why didn't you say yes?" Apollo asked. "This is important."

"Well . . ." Rocky's voice trailed off.

"Well what?"

"It's important to spend time around here, too."

Rocky glanced around his property. Even though it was in disarray, it was his home. His family's home. His fights hadn't just been for him, they had been for Adrian and Rocky Junior, too. He had earned the right to enjoy his family.

"You don't want to fight the Russian now. Is that what you're saying?"

"I'm saying, Apollo, that I'll do it when I have to. I mean I think it's about time to cut it loose."

"What?" Apollo's face was screwed up in disbelief.

"Y'know," Rocky said, calmly, "the title . . . I don't have anything more to prove."

Apollo was silent for a moment. Rocky could almost see the cogs turning inside his head, but he still didn't have the faintest idea what the end product of all that brain labor would be. But he knew Apollo was getting closer to telling him.

"This is the opportunity of a lifetime," Apollo exclaimed. "This is not just a boxing match, it's another Russian propaganda machine starting up, and they didn't forget anything. They're even trying to win the women over by having the Russian's wife talk about what a great guy this Drago is."

"Maybe he is."

It was just common sense that you didn't bring your

39

wife halfway around the world to tell everyone what a bum you were, Rocky thought. But he knew Apollo was propagandizing as much as the Russians. He just wished he'd get to the point.

"Forget it. It's politics all the way, Stallion."

Rocky smiled. "Politics? I have a hard time figuring out who to vote for. And then when they get in office I always know I made a mistake."

"Rocky, seriously. What matters is you have a chance to be more important to people than ever. You have a chance to stand face to face with their best! You'll be a symbol, man. You'll be in the history books. Look, if you don't wanna do it, I'll do it."

There it was, out in the open, the point, the purpose of the visit. Apollo wanted a last hurrah. You bet it's politics, Rocky thought, and nobody was ever better at it than you, Apollo. A grand finale. Rocky could see it. If anybody deserved it, Apollo did. But the Russian looked dangerous, an unknown factor that should be approached carefully. Yet Apollo had been—still was—a great boxer. He had years of experience that could make the difference. This wasn't an open-and-shut matter. It required some thought.

"You're the showman, Apollo."

"I wouldn't mind doing it."

They both broke out laughing at Apollo's bald understatement. He looked like he'd give up his firstborn to do it.

Rocky picked up a football that was at the statue's base.

Apollo looked at him expectantly.

"You'd be better at getting this going, Apollo."

Apollo nodded agreement.

"Why not take off your jacket and tie. We'll toss the ball around a little and think about this."

"Yo," Apollo said, dropping his jacket and tie on the ground.

"Maybe you'll work up an appetite and stay for dinner."

"I never turn down a free Italian meal. Hut one—hut two." Apollo took off running and then cut left.

Rocky let loose a long, wobbling spiral that was too far ahead of Apollo.

Apollo leaped, stretched one hand high in the air, felt the ball land in the palm of his hand, and pulled it in to him.

A performance of amazing grace.

# Chapter 5

There weren't as many reporters assembled as there had been at J.F.K. Airport, and those that had made it had much less enthusiasm. The Russians had lost their novelty effect. The media had done such a blitzkrieg on them that they had become household words. Drago and his wife Ludmilla were as familiar as rock stars. And, like a lot of overexposed personalities, they were on the verge of suffering a backlash of public opinion. So far there had been a lot of talk and no action, a lot of muscle flexing and no boxing.

Koloff had been receiving pressure from his superiors. He was the one who proposed this venture; now they wanted results from it. This was a business trip, not a vacation. Drago had better fight somebody soon or Koloff might be breaking out in sweats that no amount of cologne could cover. He had already begun to douse himself with the stuff.

This wasn't an official press conference, just an informal gathering of the media to show them how Drago trained. The training room itself was done in antiseptic operating-room white, and the Minicams were having a hard time with the glare they were picking up. There were the usual speed bags, heavy bags, and, of course, a ring. But that's where the resemblance to the average training room ended. This one looked like a cross between a laboratory and a factory. Machines of all sorts lined the walls. Most of them featured digital readouts or oscilloscope screens with wavering lines.

The media men walked around gawking at the machines. Most of them were old sportswriters and had never seen anything like this in their careers. It didn't even smell like a training room. It didn't have the feeling of a place where men pounded at each other, dripped sweat, and bled. The few who were near Koloff did detect a sweet smell that seemed incongruous with a training room. But as they had already observed, this was not a normal training room. This could well be the prototype high tech training room of the future. If that were true, they thought, it was only a matter of time before the boxers themselves were eliminated.

While the Minicams filmed away, Drago bounced around shadowboxing. He was dressed in a tank top and sweat pants. Both garments bore the hammer and sickle insignia of the Soviet Union. Attached to his back underneath the tank top were a pair of electrodes. The wires leading from the electrodes were attached to a video camera and a large computer graph with a diaphragmatic readout instrument that charted the angle of the body when it made impact with a stationary target. It made Drago look more like a robot than ever. The reporters became restless. With Drago wired up like the Six Million Dollar Man it was obvious that they hadn't been asked here to watch him shadowbox. They wondered when the action would begin.

They glanced expectantly at Ludmilla. It was obvious that she hadn't spent all her time in the training room. She was dressed in clothes from Saks—a shirt with a blouse covered by a stylishly short jacket. With her height, she resembled a model. She had the same vacuous look as most models. Koloff stood beside her, sweating. Rimsky ignored everybody but Drago. He kept watching Drago's hands and feet. Occasionally he would glance at Manuel vega, who simply nodded his head in a bored way.

Rimsky put his hand on Drago's shoulder. Drago stopped his exercise and faced the reporters.

Ludmilla cleared her throat.

"My husband and I thank you for coming to our training room today. As you can see, it is highly advanced,

43

and we wish to show the American press and television a small sample of the advances our country has made in the technology of human performance."

Most of the reporters thought that *her* performance was improving with time and practice. In their estimation, she had risen from a C+ to a B.

"Coach Rimsky," one reporter asked, "What exactly does this do to enhance performance?"

Before Rimsky could answer, Koloff interjected, "If I may answer, it makes a man a better man, a great athlete a super athlete by harnessing all his strength. Though most of the world is ignorant in body chemistry, we wish to share this with your country."

Koloff knew that his superiors would be reading the reports of the interview. He wanted to get into the limelight as much as possible. A trickle of sweat ran down his ribs.

"Well, all I see is a bunch of machines," another reporter said, "and then you talk about body chemistry. What does it mean? How does it work? Has it been proven?"

Koloff opened his mouth, but he couldn't think of a thing to say. He was a diplomat, not a sports expert, certainly not a boxing expert. He just repeated rehearsed speeches. He had no idea what the machines did.

Rimsky smiled at Koloff's discomfort. Ah, politicians, what a worthless lot. The best thing about them was that they couldn't read minds. He turned his attention to the reporter.

"Proven?" His smile became sinister.

He nodded at Drago, who wound up and threw a right-hand haymaker into a padded square that was connected to the computer. The meter in the computer flashed a digital readout: *1850*.

Rimsky looked grimly at the readout, then back at the reporter.

"A normal heavyweight averages seven hundred pounds of pressure per square inch. Drago averages 1850 pounds ... so the result's quite obvious."

"What result?" the reporter persisted.

"Whatever he hits, he destroys."

Ludmilla smiled. Koloff smiled. Rimsky smiled.

Drago, Vega, and the reporters were not smiling. Hitting a machine was one thing; hitting a man was another.

# Chapter 6

Adrian passed the dinner plates to the housekeeper, who scraped off the remnants of the lasagna dinner and slipped the plates into the little plastic holders in the dishwasher. Their movements were graceful and effortless, like soldiers unloading ammo boxes from a truck. Then a plate slipped through Adrian's fingers and crashed to the parquet floor, breaking into dangerous little pieces. Adrian shook her head glumly and bent over to pick up the fragments. The housekeeper stopped her by stepping over the fragments.

"You're not going to cut up your fingers while I'm here," the housekeeper warned. "I'll pick it up with a broom and dustpan. You get back out into the dining room where you belong. I'll take care of the kitchen."

Adrian smiled and put her hand on the housekeeper's shoulder. "You're right. I'm no help out here. Not tonight."

The housekeeper, Mrs. Tulio, had been with the Balboas since Rocky Junior was born and considered herself an integral part of the household. She was right.

"They're up to something out there, aren't they?" Mrs. Tulio asked.

"I'm not sure, but I've got a feeling."

"Don't worry about it," the housekeeper assured her. "They're just men. They talk more than they do."

Adrian nodded in agreement, but she didn't feel reassured. She started toward the dining room.

The phone rang. Adrian picked up the kitchen extension.

"Cora?" A pause. "Yes, he's here. Do you want to talk to him?" Another pause, but longer. "Oh, I see...."

Adrian's face was troubled and thoughtful.

When Adrian entered the dining room Apollo was pacing alongside the dinner table like a wildcat in a cage. She had seen him like this before—face aglow, hands wildly gesticulating, body emitting energy that was as tangible as sparks. She was never able to tell for sure where the show ended and Apollo began. He could be a wily con man delivering the big hype, as he had been in the Centennial bout, or he could be a compassionate assistant, as he was in helping Rocky against Clubber Lang. She sincerely liked Apollo, but she was wary of him. Things happened when he was around. He made them happen. Adrian was in favor of a more sedentary life. She didn't want to be bored, but she felt that she had already been through more than her share of excitement. She wanted to be able to look forward to tomorrow without anxiety. The quiet pet shop had been torn down, but a piece of it still existed in her.

Apollo felt high. His stomach was full of some of the best lasagna he had ever eaten. His head felt as if it were crackling with electricity. Energy surged through him like a lava flow. He couldn't stand still. His legs were moving of their own volition.

"The Russians know the division is damned weak now and they can stomp their way up the ranks if nobody tries to stop them," Apollo said, moving restlessly, as if he were in a boxing ring waiting for an opponent. "When that happens they'll start laying on the talk about who's superior again. I saw this boy box during the Olympics."

Apollo had journeyed to Russia as a sportscaster during the boycotted 1980 Olympic Games. It hadn't been one of the highlights of his life. He had liked the people— the ones that he had met in the streets, not his official escorts. The escorts had been cold, efficient watchdogs without names. He had felt like he was in a prison. He could do certain things, go certain places, then suddenly he would be stopped. It was like a dog having his chain jerked. If that wasn't bad enough, he was constantly embarrassed by the preferential treatment that he and the other foreigners received at restaurants and other public places. He had seen discrimination before and he didn't like being a participant in it. He had been glad to get back to the States.

"He's strong, but clumsy," Apollo said pointedly, grinning. "Kinda like somebody else I used to know." Then back to business: "I can beat him. I know I can beat him."

He had to beat him. Apollo knew, as all fighters knew, that you could win forty fights in a long, hard-fought career and the public would only remember the last fight—the one you lost. The one that took the championship belt away from you. The one that made you an ex-athlete if you were smart or a cauliflowered, punch-drunk bum on carnival circuits if you didn't quit. Apollo didn't like either option. He knew he had one last fight in him. He had proved that to himself when he had boxed Rocky at Goldmill's Gym.

Rocky looked at Adrian. He could feel her eyes watching him. It wasn't a signal, just an awareness, a kind of mental telepathy. It would have been the same even if they had been in different rooms. He could see little crow's-feet around her eyes, but he knew they were there because of worry, not age. Rocky knew she didn't like the conversation. She didn't have to say anything to tell him that. She looked vulnerable. And beautiful. What eyes, Rocky thought.

"Why do you want to fight?" Adrian asked. It was the same question that had been running through her head for years. She had never gotten a truly comprehensible answer. She didn't expect one this time. But she never gave up. She wanted to understand.

Apollo's face was a study in surprise and disbelief, but it passed quickly. Cora had already asked him the question. He hadn't been able to explain it to her, so there was no point in attempting to answer Adrian. She wouldn't comprehend. He wasn't sure if he did. He looked at Rocky for support. He couldn't read his friend's expression.

"Let's just say it's something I believe in."

Let's just call that an evasion, Adrian thought.

Paulie was halfheartedly listening to the conversation while devouring a massive bowl of Neapolitan ice cream, and meticulously studying the centerfold in the new issue of *Playboy*. The ice cream wasn't the only edible thing on his mind. There were more things in the world than Russians and boxing. Art, for example.

Rocky Junior knew something important was happening, but he didn't know what it was. Apollo didn't come for dinner except on special occasions. And his mom and dad seemed to be acting strange. Not very strange, but different. Someday he'd understand adults, but this wasn't the day.

Rocky turned to him. "You can get ready for bed."

Rocky Junior knew it was a command, not a privilege.

"Okay. Good night, Daddy," he said, kissing his father. Rocky Junior worked his way around the table kissing Paulie (and catching a glimpse of the centerfold), then Apollo, who hugged him tightly, and finally his mother. She picked him up and gave him a big squeeze and a warm kiss. He felt good. He had the best parents in the whole world.

Paulie took a last lingering look at the Playmate, then laid the magazine on the table. It was time for him to leave his fantasy world.

"Your only uncle wishes you sweet dreams." But not the same variety that Paulie would be having.

"Night, big man," Apollo joined in.

Rocky Junior beamed and said good night to both of them, then went into the kitchen to say the same to Mrs. Tulio. She'd feel neglected if he didn't and besides, she smelled good.

"Yo. Don't you think people are expecting Rocky to whack this bum out first?" Paulie said to Apollo.

Rocky remained silent, looking intently at Adrian.

"Why ain't you fighting, Rock?" Paulie continued.

"'Cause he's doing me a favor," Apollo explained.

"What's the purpose?" Adrian demanded. "What is worth getting hurt for at this point in your life?"

Everyone was silent, surprised, and uncomfortable with her outburst.

Paulie decided that this was a situation that demanded a beer. He pushed the button on his remote control. A moment later the robot wheeled in from the kitchen carrying a bottle of beer and a glass. Paulie took a bottle opener from the folds of the apron that was tied around

48

the robot and snapped off the bottle cap in a professional manner.

"What's that?" Apollo exclaimed.

"My new girl," Paulie said, pouring the beer in the glass. He turned to the robot. "Thanks, honey."

"Yes, handsome," the robot droned. "You are the greatest. See you sport."

"Who taught it to talk like that?" Rocky asked. This was an unplanned-for development. He had only bought the robot as a joke. It seemed to turning into more than a machine.

"Comes natural," Paulie said slyly. He pushed the remote control button again and the robot wheeled back into the kitchen.

Apollo shook his head in wonder, then got back to the business at hand.

"See, I don't want this bum coming over here with their hype trying to make us look bad. They try every other way. But with Rock's help, we'll get great media coverage and make them look bad for a change."

It was hard to tell if Adrian was angry or sad, but she was definitely upset. The way she looked at Rocky and Apollo made them uncomfortable.

"Apollo, you've been retired for nearly five years. Don't you think it's time to think about something else? I mean, how much more can you take? Either of you?" She felt her stomach tightening up. If she stayed in the room much longer she would get a headache. "Nice seeing you again," she said to Apollo as she went into the kitchen.

Apollo hadn't planned on this complication. He had expected it from his wife, but not from Adrian. It wasn't as if he were trying to get Rocky to fight. It was the exact opposite. If Rocky fought, Apollo was out in the cold.

"Are you with me?" Apollo wanted to know.

Rocky looked toward the kitchen, confusion evident on his face.

"Be right back," Rocky said, rising.

Adrian was putting away the last of the food, stuffing leftovers in Tupperware containers and making sure the lids snapped on tightly. Mrs. Tulio was still stacking dishes in the dishwasher. Adrian opened the refrigerator door and placed the containers inside.

Rocky wondered if the chill in the kitchen was coming from the refrigerator.

"Adrian, you mad over this?"

"Not mad," she reflected. "I just have bad feelings about it."

She took a carton of milk and squeezed it in next to the food containers.

"You shouldn't. Apollo just has this great imagination."

Adrian shut the fridge and faced Rocky.

"It is imagination. Rocky, don't you see? Apollo just can't stand being forgotten, but it's something he's got to face. You'll have to, too."

Rocky let the last comment slip by. He had thought about it, but he didn't want to dwell on it. Especially now.

"I don't think it's about that. I think he really believes in what he's saying."

Adrian looked thoughtful. She knew Rocky's gut instincts had a lot of validity, but they were talking about Apollo Creed, a man of many facades. So many that maybe even Apollo didn't know who the real Apollo Creed was.

"Maybe he does. But this won't happen if you don't back it. Don't you see that he thinks he's fighting for the whole country? Rocky, it's not the Dark Ages, when tribes sent out their best fighters to kill each other. We're supposed to be a little civilized. His reasons for fighting this time are wrong. It's more like a bad publicity stunt."

"I'll talk some more to him."

"You should," Adrian agreed. "You're his friend and now is when a friend is needed. Talk to him. Let him know he's not the Lone Ranger. He's a married man. He should consider that, too."

"I'll talk to him. I don't know what I'm going to say, but I'll talk to him."

"That's good enough for me." Adrian kissed him lightly on the lips. "I'm going upstairs to read."

Adrian walked out of the kitchen.

Rocky stood there wondering what he was going to say to Apollo. Suddenly it became fascinating to watch the housekeeper finish up her chores. It was a convenient distraction, momentarily keeping his thoughts away from Apollo. Mrs. Tulio felt the attention she was getting and looked questioningly at Rocky.

"Don't mind me." He smiled. "It's a weird night."

She went back to her duties, puzzled.

Hell, what was he worried about? Rocky thought. Apollo would probably do all the talking.

Apollo came out of his corner, took a deep breath, and started circling to the left. He flicked three jabs, then two hard rights into Rocky's face. Creed switched directions, threw two more jabs, a right, a left, then missed.

Rocky jumped forward and put all his weight behind a left hook that nearly knocked Creed off his feet. The champion's eyes glassed over and he tried to backpedal but succeeded only in staggering. Rocky moved in and connected with three more hooks, then a right, then another left. Creed swayed and almost went down. Then Apollo froze, leaning at a forty-five degree angle.

"Too bad I couldn't do that during the match," Apollo said, relaxing on the couch as he and Rocky watched a videocassette recording of their rematch at the Spectrum. "Unfreeze me, Rocky. I still got a few good punches left."

Rocky worked the remote control and the fight continued.

Rocky moved in and connected with a left hook to the body that made the champ fall back against the ropes. Rocky closed in for the knockout and was greeted by a stiff right hand. It was followed by a series of blows that caused Rocky's legs to buckle. Punch after punch cascaded off Rocky's demolished face. He stumbled but wouldn't fall.

"This was one good fight," Apollo commented.

"A tough one," Rocky agreed.

"I'm getting brain damage just watching it. Look at that!"

A right hook slammed into Apollo's head, causing sweat to fly off him in a spray.

"Y'know, isn't it something how people care when you're in that ring and they care when you're bleeding, but soon as you step out of that ring nobody cares? You're ancient history."

"You're not ancient history, Apollo."

"I'm getting there." Apollo glanced at the large-screen television set and watched himself slip past one of Rocky's righthanders and counter with a solid jab that jarred Rocky.

51

"Nice punch, Apollo," he mused.

"Apollo, I wanna say something."

"What?"

"Maybe you don't wanna hear this."

"Hear what?"

"This fight against the Russian, you think maybe it's not against him?"

Apollo laughed. "Then who's it against?"

"You against you, isn't it?"

Rocky was glad he had said it, had finally gotten it out in the open where it could be examined. He pushed a button on the remote and the television screen went blank. The past had its place, but right now Rocky wanted to concentrate on the present.

"You're really getting punchy, Rocky."

"C'mon," Rocky said earnestly. "Everybody knows you were a great fighter, and I guess maybe the hardest thing to admit is when the show is over."

Apollo looked patiently at Rocky, almost like a teacher contending with a errant but likable schoolboy.

"When you think it's over, it is. I'm not ready to roll over and play dead. Are you? You don't think it's over, do you?"

Rocky thought about the question. Did he? Was he ready to step out of the ring?

"I don't know," he answered truthfully. "Soon somebody's gonna take it away, just like I did to you. Getting beat is all part of it."

"That's crazy!"

"A good champ should win it and lose it in the ring, like you did."

"Then what?" Apollo threw his hands up in a gesture of frustration. "Where do we go? 'Cause we sure as hell can't be born again."

"No. But we can change," Rocky said, calmly.

"I don't wanna change. I like who I am. You think I want this fight to happen because I feel forgotten? You think this is some kind of ego trip?"

"I feel the same way you do, Apollo. I feel like maybe we're changing into a different kind of guy. Not as hungry or as popular." Rocky switched the VCR back on and color flowed onto the TV screen. Rocky and Apollo were back battling it out. Rocky pointed to the two figures on the screen. "We both gotta face it: that's not us anymore. We're not what we were. We're changing into regular people."

Apollo rose from the couch and stood in front of the television set, blocking it from view. He wanted Rocky to know that he was still here, he was still viable, he wasn't just an image in a fight from the past.

"No!" he said forcefully. "Stallion, you may think you're changing, but what you really are doesn't change. Forget all this money and stuff you got around you. It doesn't change anything! You and me, we don't have a choice. You can dress a wolf up to look tame, but underneath he's still a wolf and he'll tear you apart! We're born with a killer instinct that can never be tamed. We can't turn it off like some radio. We have to go the limit, Rocky, we have to live on the edge, we have to have the action because we're the warriors! We have to push ourselves more and more because without a challenge, without a damned war to fight, the warrior may as well be dead, too! I'm not ready to lie down yet, Rocky. Are you?"

Rocky had to admit that Apollo did look like a warrior. A well-dressed one, but a warrior nonetheless. Maybe he could take the Russian. It would just be an exhibition match. There wouldn't be the blood lust of a championship bout. Apollo had come through for Rocky in the dark days after Mickey's death. He had revitalized him, snapped him out of his self-pity. Then, in California, he had shown him the eye of the tiger.

That's what Rocky saw now as he looked at Apollo. The eye of the tiger, burning bright.

He's your friend, and now he needs a friend. Adrian's words echoed in Rocky's head, but not in the way she had meant them. Apollo was asking for help. Friends helped each other. It was that simple.

"When do we start?" Rocky asked.

# Chapter 7

It was another press conference. Two tables lined with microphones were at the head of the hall facing empty folding chairs that would soon hold reporters. The hall was quiet, tomblike. The janitor had finished setting up the folding chairs an hour ago and was now off in a private alcove finishing up his morning pint of Ignorant Willy, otherwise known as I.W. Harper. He'd be back in the hall soon because he wanted to see the champ and Mr. Creed. They meant something to him. He had watched both of them fight for years. He felt that he knew them. Their victories had made up for his failures. He felt that he had shared something with them. Life.

Two presidents had held press conferences in this hall. They had talked about life, liberty, and the pursuit of happiness. They had said the expected and done the expected and sought reelection. No excitement there, just the same old stale manure that emanated from all politicians since politics had become a vocation instead of an avocation. Today would be different. It wouldn't be just rhetoric put on the line. The talk would be about flesh and blood. Substance. A nice change. Like another coat of varnish.

* * *

Rocky and Apollo sat at the smaller of the two tables. Apollo's face was beaming. This was just like the good old times. He didn't even mind the blinding glare that came from what seemed like a wall of Minicams. He thought of it as just another kind of spotlight. This was the day he had been waiting for ever since he had watched the news show from his hammock. God, he felt good.

Rocky wasn't in the same humor. Adrian hadn't said ten words to him before he left the house. She was still upset about the exhibition match. He had tried to explain to her that Apollo had been in his corner when he needed him and it was time to return the favor. She didn't buy it. She felt that that had been different. He told her it had been the same. He had been fighting for his self-esteem, and Apollo was doing the same thing now. It was necessary that Rocky help him.

The atmosphere wasn't improved by a phone call from Cora. Adrian was talking to her when he left. Rocky Junior had been the only one to say goodbye to him. Paulie had been partying with his robot the night before and was still sleeping it off. The walk from the house to the car had been a lonely one. The weather hadn't helped, either. It had been cold and overcast. Rocky wasn't happy this morning, but he had given Apollo his word and he was going to keep it.

The four Russians sat at the other table. Behind them stood plainclothes Russian security agents. Their faces were expressionless as they constantly scanned the hall looking for odd movements or a glimpse of a gun that would propel them into action. In contrast, Drago, Ludmilla, Rimsky, and Koloff were smiling and comfortably fielding questions from the reporters. They were even laughing at Apollo's colorful answers. They had spent a long time practicing for this conference and they were giving a good performance.

The reporters were up for this session after days of being lulled into boredom at the frequent conferences held by the Russians. Even Ludmilla didn't look as good to them as she had initially. Drago was the only one who still held a measure of fascination for them. A mountain is a mountain; time doesn't change that.

The last vestiges of hangovers had left most of the reporters, and they were warming up to the question-and-answer session. Rocky and Apollo were always good copy, and even the Russians seemed to be getting the knack of handling the media.

The janitor leaned against the wall in a back corner, enjoying the show even though it looked a little blurred to him.

"Apollo!" one of the reporters shouted.

Apollo looked around.

"Over here, please," the reporter called.

Apollo found the voice and recognized the face that went with it.

"Yo." He smiled.

"Apollo, what made you decide to put on an exhibition fight with Drago?"

"I thought it would be a nice way to get acquainted."

Rocky was beginning to feel better. Apollo's vitality was affecting him, too. This couldn't be wrong. It had been a while since he had seen Apollo enjoying himself so much.

"Apollo, isn't Drago a little inexperienced to be in the same ring with you?"

Apollo looked Drago straight in the eyes. "We'll be polite and box real easy."

There was a general murmur of laughter in the room. These reporters had appreciated Apollo for more years than they wanted to remember. Drago gave his best tight-lipped smile.

"So no quick knockout predictions?" another reporter yelled, managing to make himself heard.

"No, I'm not mad at him." The intensity in Apollo's eyes belied his statement. "It's just an exhibition to have fun and get to know each other."

Drago didn't look like someone who wanted to make new friends.

"Rocky, are you helping to train Apollo?"

"I'm gonna try."

"What do you mean—try?" Apollo said, an exaggerated look of reproach and astonishment creasing his face.

"You're very hard to keep in one place." Rocky smiled, appreciating Apollo's setup. Maybe they could put an act together after this was over and have Rocky Junior film them.

Even the Russians emitted friendly laughter. The reporters turned to them.

"Drago, how does it feel to spar with the great former champion?"

Drago smiled and turned to his wife with a look of childlike innocence on his face. He didn't quite pull it off, but he came close. He and Ludmilla whispered some words in Russian.

Ludmilla turned to the reporter and addressed him very soothingly. "My husband is very happy to have this opportunity. It's his dream."

Apollo nudged Rocky in the ribs and whispered to him, "Mine, too."

"In my country," Ludmilla continued, "Apollo Creed is well known and highly respected."

Now it was Rocky's turn. "They don't know you very well, Apollo."

Apollo choked silently on his laughter. They were beginning to act like schoolboys. It was a good feeling. Rocky wished that Adrian were here. Maybe it would help to allay her fears.

"My husband has read much about Apollo Creed and Champion Balboa. They are his idols. This is a dream come true for him."

The reporters stirred uneasily. She was beginning to lay it on too thick again. It sounded like a rehearsed, memorized reading. Just when they began to like her she started sounding mechanical.

Hoping to get her away from her script a reporter said, "Ludmilla, you've won two world medals in swimming. Any more competitions for you?"

"No, I'll stay dry a while, thank you."

"What do you do to stay in shape nowadays?"

Apollo couldn't pass it up. He saw the punch line coming. He said to Rocky in a low voice, "Shopping."

Right on cue Ludmilla answered, "I shop."

The laughter was there, but it was polite, formal. They had all heard the line before. But Ludmilla was by far the most likable of the quartet, and any attempts she made to loosen up were appreciated.

A reporter waved his hand in frustration until Rimsky nodded at him.

"Does Drago think he can do well against an experienced champion?"

Rimsky and Drago had a hurried conference in Russian as they discussed the questions. They both emerged smiling.

"He hopes Apollo Creed does not hit him too hard, because he bruises easily," Rimsky said slyly.

More laughter, even louder than before, because there wasn't a single person in the room who believed Drago had come up with that line. The reporters would have an even better laugh about it over a drink after the conference ended. Rimsky wore a pleased, self-satisfied look that added to the laughter.

"What about rumors that Drago is a type of Soviet Superman?"

"Yes, he is strong, but he is inexperienced," Rimsky answered, pleased that the cameras were trained on him.

Apollo looked at Rocky. "They're trying to set me up." Rocky nodded. It was a good tactic—trying to give Apollo a false sense of security and at the same time leaving themselves an escape hatch if Drago didn't make a good showing.

"What's Drago like about America so far?"

Koloff had been feeling neglected. After all, he was the one with the diplomatic training. This was supposed to be his specialty. Besides, a little camera exposure wouldn't hurt him. He never knew when his superiors were watching. The match with Creed had stopped his excessive perspiring, but he knew that a man in his position always had to be careful, prepared for anything. He quickly jumped in to field the question before anyone else could.

"He likes what anyone likes—the opportunity to prove oneself. We also would like to thank the people and the press for being so gracious." The statement was a little unctuous, but at least he was on the record for saying something.

A reporter in the front row decided it was time for the questioning to get a little tougher. He was tired of the kid glove approach to the Russians. It was time to get down to bare knuckles.

"There have been many rumors about blood doping, synthetic growth hormones, and widespread distribution

58

of anabolic steroids in the Soviet Union for the sole purpose of creating the super athlete. Has Drago ever taken part in these experiments?"

The tension level in the room increased dramatically. Koloff and Rimsky tried to stare the reporter down, their eyes dark and malevolent. But the reporter held his ground, his eyes never wavering from theirs. He had once conducted an interview alone in a room with a serial murderer who had twenty-four kills to his credit. The Russians didn't bother him.

"Well?" the reporter persisted.

Ludmilla saved the day. She turned on her best smile and said charmingly, "Like your Popeye, he just ate spinach every day."

The reporter laughed as loudly as everyone else. He gave credit where it was due. She was faster on her feet than he had expected.

"No," Ludmilla continued in a more serious tone, "Ivan is a natural athlete."

Natural athletes were kids in school, Rocky thought, who played just for the pure joy and hell of it. When you became a pro or even a dedicated amateur all that changed. Training became the most important part of your life. You tortured yourself to get into shape. It wasn't natural to enter an arena where, if you prospered, you would eventually have your ribs broken, your nose flattened and smeared over your face, maybe have your vision impaired, and, worst of all, suffer so many concussions that your thought processes became permanently altered. No, Drago wasn't a natural athlete. None of them were. They lived a different life than other people did. Natural, normal—these words didn't apply to full-time athletes. He wasn't sure why they did it. It was more than money, he knew that. But he didn't know the full reason. If he did, he would be able to answer a lot of questions about himself. He could share more with Adrian.

Another question came from the reporters.

"Why do you all travel with so many bodyguards?"

The security men either didn't understand English or they were practicing to be statues. They just stood there, still and silent.

"Bodyguards?" Koloff said with charming amazement that ended in a smile. "No, these men are more like chaperons and friends who help us adjust to a new life-style in a new country."

Even Koloff felt a tinge of embarrassment at that explanation.

Apollo snorted and said to himself, "Gimme a break."

Rocky just shook his head in wonder. These people could at least keep up with Apollo in the baloney department. He hoped the press conference would end soon. He didn't know how much more he could take.

One of the photographers stood up and walked toward the tables. The bodyguards stirred nervously. Koloff motioned at them to be still. They resumed their former poses. Marble men.

"Apollo, could you and Drago stand for some pictures?" the photographer asked.

Apollo looked at Drago, who nodded agreement. Rocky wondered why Drago could understand English perfectly at some times and seemed to have no knowledge of it at other times. Probably a matter of convenience.

"Thought you'd never ask," Apollo said, smiling.

Apollo tugged at Rocky's arm and they walked over and met Drago between the tables. Rocky felt a crick in his neck as he looked up at Drago. Maybe Adrian had a point. Drago wasn't the Empire State Building, but he had size.

"Tall structure, isn't he?" Rocky mumbled to Apollo.

Apollo just looked at Drago and smiled. The bigger they are, the harder they fall. Apollo believed in clichés—that was why he used them so much.

Drago looked down at Apollo and Rocky, his smile masking his thoughts. He wouldn't have to box Creed. He could just step on him and squash him like a cockroach.

Apollo and Drago struck friendly boxing poses, but their eyes were steely.

"Rocky, how do you think Apollo should fight Drago?"

The photographers moved into their various positions. Rocky glanced up at Drago, then turned sharply to the reporter who had asked the question.

"With a ladder."

Flash bars started exploding.

Click.

The janitor folded and stacked the chairs. The hall was his again. The only noise in it was the creaking of the chairs. He had a lot to tell his friends. He had been close to celebrities. In his neighborhood, that made him a celebrity. He hurried with the chairs. It was time for his afternoon pint.

# Chapter 8

Las Vegas.

Just the name sparkled brightly in the minds of most people, much like the miles of neon that kept the city in perpetual daylight. It was known all over the world yet it really didn't have any reason to exist. At least not in the normal way that certain towns came into existence because of fertile land that could produce crops, or natural resources that made them develop into industrial centers, or a location near a bay that was perfect for a seaport. Las Vegas had none of those things. All it had was people. And legalized gambling.

It was an oasis of green in the middle of a vast brown desert. In Spanish, *las vegas* means "the meadows." The Spanish lost the town to the Mexicans, who in turn lost it to the United States. Lost, stolen—the words were interchangeable in this case. A few decades ago Las Vegas was just another small western town with a few casinos waiting to take your money. But they were small casinos that were vulnerable to going bust themselves. Then a big change occurred. It was brought about by a gangster named Bugsy Siegel who had a vision of creating a paradise in the desert. With the assistance of some dubious business associates on the east coast and some friends in Hollywood, Siegel built the Flamingo Hotel. The hotel was fabulous, a sight to behold, but it proved unlucky for

Siegel. The Flamingo lost money. Lots of money. Siegel lost his life and part of his head. But his dream lived on. More and more elaborate hotels and casinos were built. Las Vegas became a billion-dollar enterprise. Fortunes were won or lost in minutes—mainly lost. The town grew on the money of the losers.

But they kept coming, some with systems that couldn't lose or secret skills that couldn't be detected. It really didn't matter if they won or lost. They kept coming. And gambling. On anything.

It was the perfect place for a boxing match. It was where Apollo and Drago were going to fight.

The plane descended from the clear blue sky onto the landing strip at McCarren Airport. Rocky, Apollo, Paulie, and Duke sat silently in the first-class section of the plane, each lost in his own thoughts. Adrian had gone to California before the Lang fight because she thought she could help Rocky. There wouldn't have been any purpose in her coming to Vegas. Rocky didn't need help—he was giving it. She could spend her time better by staying at home and taking care of Rocky Junior. She and Cora were going to fly out for the fight. She owed that to Apollo. And to Cora. Rocky was going to miss his wife, but he knew the hard training would give him little time to think about her.

Apollo felt electricity running through his body. This was his kind of town, nonstop twenty-four-hour action. And for a few days he was going to be the center of attention. Maybe the slot machine players wouldn't be distracted by him, but others would.

Paulie couldn't wait to hit the casinos. He had heard about Las Vegas for years, but this was his first visit. He knew it was going to be a memorable one. Duke was pensive. In his mind he kept seeing the massive build of Drago. It wasn't a reassuring image.

They deplaned and pressed through the waiting photographers and reporters. Time was short and Rocky didn't want to waste any of it on press conferences. Some of the reporters were confused, others angry. This wasn't what they had expected of the champ and Apollo. But the entourage continued to plow ahead. Paulie paused long enough to put a quarter in a slot machine. The machine whirred as he pulled the handle, and then there was a clatter as coins fell into the tray at the bottom of the machine. Paulie pocketed the money. It was a good omen. He was going to make a big splash in this town.

A limousine was waiting for them. They got in and were taken to the MGM Grand Hotel. As they arrived they could see a giant banner draped across the front of the hotel. When they got out of the limo they read the banner: WELCOME APOLLO CREED. A bellboy took their bags.

Rocky and Apollo looked at each other.

Now the work would begin.

The hotel had closed down the ballroom where the fight was going to take place and Rocky was using it as their training quarters. The ring had already been erected and decorators were putting up paper bunting. Rocky wondered what Mickey would think of this setup. He smiled to himself as he imagined Mickey grousing and complaining. The heavy bag, the speed bag, and all the other training paraphernalia were set up. It would do, Rocky thought. But equipment was the least important part of training. Apollo had taught him that in Los Angeles.

The boxers he had met in the Main Street Gym were poorly equipped and financed. Many of them worked full-time jobs and still managed to get in four or five hours of training a day. They did it because they wanted to. Their eyes had a hungry look. They were fighting for their dreams and they were doing it the only way they knew how, with their fists. Apollo had accused Rocky of losing that fierce desire. His years as champion had made him soft, content. And Apollo had been right. Now Rocky wondered if the same thing had happened to Apollo. Did Apollo still have the eye of the tiger? Or had he fooled Rocky? He'd find out soon.

The Russians were training in a camp outside of town. It was closed to the public. So much for wanting to share their scientific breakthroughs with the American athletes. They had even stopped giving press conferences, a development for which everybody was grateful. It was as if they had vanished. All the hoopla was gone. They had gotten down to business.

That was fine with Rocky. It was exactly what he wanted to do, too.

Onlookers jammed the ballroom floor. Rocky eyed them with displeasure, as Mickey would have done. They were a necessary distraction, though. He could hardly expect the Grand to be rude to guests. Las Vegas was all about money, and that's what these people had brought with them. At times Rocky spotted Paulie wandering among the spectators. This time he wasn't a vendor dispensing hats and other memorabilia, as he had during Rocky's first fight with Clubber Lang. He was too dignified for that now. He was Apollo's public relations man. The fact that there wasn't any public relations work to do didn't bother Paulie. It delighted him. It gave him more time to spend in the casinos. He had discovered that the casinos had almost as many beautiful women as they had one-armed bandits. His only regret was that he hadn't been able to bring his robot with him. He actually missed it. Luckily, everywhere he looked there were beautiful waitresses with free beers on their trays.

Apollo jumped rope in time to the music that was blaring from a portable cassette player. He jumped lightly, always staying on the balls of his feet. It was like watching a ballet dancer. He made it seem effortless. Playing to the crowd, he would do various routines with the rope, jumping backwards, crisscrossing his arms, then pouring on the speed until sweat popped from his forehead and the rope blurred into a translucent bubble that enclosed him. The crowd loved it. They broke into little flurries of applause. Apollo beamed with pleasure. It was like a love affair. Apollo took a little bow in the direction of his admirers. More laughter and scattered applause.

"Let's get back to business, Apollo," Rocky said, his voice expressing disapproval.

Apollo looked at him curiously but resumed his jumping. Some of the spectators started to clap their hands in time to the music. Apollo escalated his speed.

Rocky scowled as he looked at his stopwatch. What was happening to him? He hadn't liked the tone in his voice when he spoke to Apollo. It had reminded him of someone, yet he couldn't remember who. After this fight he was going to stick with being a boxer and let someone else be the trainer. He was used to being told what to do, not giving the instructions. Suddenly it occurred to him whom he had sounded like: Mickey Goldmill. Rocky had trained in a circus atmosphere for the first Clubber Lang fight, and Mickey had criticized him for it. He warned him that every fight should be taken seriously because the man you stepped into the ring with wanted to beat you, to knock you out. There wasn't a boxer alive who could afford to be overconfident. And Mickey had been right.

Rocky wished Mickey were here now. He needed his help. He looked at the stopwatch again, then back at Apollo.

"Pick it up, Apollo. Move those feet faster. This isn't a disco!"

But it did resemble one, and Rocky knew it.

Apollo and his sparring partner chased each other around the ring. Their protective headgear made them look like seminude football players. The sparring partner was three inches taller than Apollo and had twenty pounds on him. They were old friends. Apollo had beaten the boxer on his way up to the championship. Sparring partners fell into two categories: hungry young bloods on the way up, looking to pick up an education; and over-the-hill mustangs who didn't want to let go, who still had a trick or two that made them special.

Apollo was moving faster than his partner, bouncing lightly on the balls of his feet, cutting his opponent's ring space down while keeping a stinging left jab constantly in his face. The big fighter set his feet, slipped the jab, and penetrated Apollo's defense with a strong right. If the fighter had thrown the same punch five years ago it might have been a knockout punch. As it was it earned him some respect from Apollo, who backed off and started circling the ring, giving the man more room.

Rocky watched intently, wondering if the right had been able to do some damage or if Apollo was just being lazy. Either way, it wasn't a good situation.

"Go on after him! Chase him down!" Rocky yelled.

Instead, Apollo turned and waved at Rocky, his mouthpiece clearly visible as he smiled.

The bystanders chuckled. Apollo was as good as any entertainer on the Strip.

Rocky shook his head, disturbed.

"C'mon, let's do it!" he urged.

Apollo nodded his head in agreement and started stalking his opponent. He began pounding the body with short, powerful jabs to the ribs and kidneys. The sparring partner started to hang onto Apollo, his breath coming in sharp, stentorian wheezes. Apollo let him hang and continued the grueling body punches. The bigger man finally managed to push Apollo away, but before he could backpedal out of striking distance Apollo lunged forward, connecting with a hard left jab to the jaw. It hurt. The sparring partner felt it all the way down to his tailbone. He curled up in a crouch, attempting to protect himself while he recovered. Apollo straightened him up with a sharp uppercut. The man started giving new thought to retiring. Maybe he had played out all his tricks. Apollo faked a left, then cut loose with a roundhouse right that connected with a resounding smack to the left side of his friend's face. Apollo's friend saw it coming, heard it hit, but never felt it. He didn't even feel the mat when he landed on it.

The next thing he knew, Apollo and Rocky were standing over him—at least, that's who he thought they were; his vision was a little blurred. Finally it cleared, and he saw Rocky holding four fingers in front of his face. Rocky's voice sounded like something filtered through a cloud, but the man knew he was being asked how many fingers he saw.

"Four," he answered.

Rocky and Apollo helped him to his feet. He was shaken but okay.

"I got a little overenthusiastic," Apollo said.

The sparring partner smiled and nodded his head. It was okay. It was what he got paid for.

Apollo took off his headgear.

"That's good enough."

Rocky looked at his watch. It was barely past one in the afternoon. Apollo was still scheduled to work on the speed bag. Rocky was even holding the special four-ounce gloves in his right hand.

"What?" Rocky said in amazement.

Apollo climbed through the ropes and left the ring.

"Let's get some air."

The way Apollo said it made it final. His day was over. He had made a strong showing and he was content with it.

Rocky helped the sparring partner out of the ring. He was a nice guy, but even on his best day he wouldn't have posed a problem for Ivan Drago. Rocky hoped Apollo wasn't losing his perspective.

"It's not going right," Duke said, getting up from one of the chairs that had been set up at ringside. "But don't worry. He'll straighten up. It's just his style."

Rocky hoped Duke was right. After all, Duke had known Apollo a lot longer than Rocky had. If anybody could figure Apollo out, it was Duke. He had been in Apollo's corner from the very start of his career. He had watched him train for many fights.

Rocky shrugged and tossed the speed bag gloves to Duke.

Tomorrow was another day.

The sun hung in the sky like a blistering orange fireball. Even with sunglasses on it was hard to look at it. The reflection of the sunlight off the water in the swimming pool was blinding. The air was hot, dry, and still. Paulie realized why people spent most of their time indoors: the climate was more than inhospitable. But there were rewards. The beauties around the pool were a pleasure to look at if one didn't mind perpetually squinting.

Paulie took a sip of a beer that had been cold two minutes ago but was now tepid. He raised his hand to signal for another one. Beside him, dressed in a bathing suit, Apollo was charming the people ringing the pool with a constant line of chatter.

"I'm gonna be crushin' the Russian."

"Get there early or you might be too late."

It was his usual stream of one-liners and they were meeting with the usual success. Apollo stretched out in his poolside chair and let his body soak up the sun's rays as he continued to talk and sign autographs. This was the life. This was what he had been missing since Rocky had taken his championship away in 1976.

A shadow loomed over him, blocking out the sunlight.

He looked up. Rocky had a determined look on his face. Apollo sighed. Rocky was taking this way too seriously.

Apollo rose from his chair and addressed the people around him. "Everybody come see the fight. It's gonna be good entertainment. As much of a delight to the eyes as I am."

People chuckled and said words of encouragement.

Rocky merely said, "Let's go."

Still smiling and waving, Apollo followed Rocky back into the hotel.

Paulie's beer arrived in its plastic cup. This one wasn't tepid, it was warm.

Another day. Apollo's ankles jerked against the incline board's foot strap. Rocky stood over him, counting. Apollo's sweaty upper torso rose in yet another sit-up. He touched his head to his knees and lowered himself with a groan. Again. And again. Apollo had lost count. It was like being flogged to the point where you no longer felt it. His breathing was labored. The veins on his forehead stood out like highways on a road map. Up and down. Up and down. Each sit-up was slower than the previous one.

"Fight it. Fight yourself. Get your mind set. Let your body know who's in control," Rocky urged.

The sweat was stinging Apollo's eyes, almost blinding him. Through a haze he saw Rocky waving him on for one more sit-up, then another and another. Apollo didn't know how many more he had left in him. He didn't even know how many he had done. It had been a long time since he had subjected his body to this kind of torture. When's this going to be over? he thought. He wanted to get back to the pool, to feel the sun being kind to his body.

"Get mean," Rocky said enthusiastically, but his expression showed a growing concern.

Apollo struggled up, touched his forehead to his knees, then collapsed on the exercise mat.

Rocky silently looked down at him.

Paulie stood at the two-dollar blackjack table. His face looked glum. The town wasn't living up to his expectations. The slot machines, after their initial payoff at the airport, had robbed him. He had sunk coins of every denomination into them and come up with more lemons than he knew existed. Then he had gotten wise and watched other players pumping coins into the machines without luck. Then, after enough money had been lost, Paulie would go over to the machine, certain that it was time for a payoff. Same results. Lemons. All he had ended up with was a tired arm and a dirty hand. Now he realized why the addicted slot machine players wore gloves. It saved your skin.

A chair opened up at the table. Paulie decided that a change of games would help his luck. He sat down and bought twenty dollars' worth of chips. If you're gonna do it, might as well splurge. He put a two-dollar chip in front of him. The dealer drew the cards out of the shoe. Paulie got a ten and a king. He suppressed a smile as he shook his head at the dealer. The dealer turned over his bottom card. A jack. Paulie thought it went well with the six that was already showing. The dealer took his mandatory hit. A five. Paulie groaned. The next time he put up a five-dollar chip. He got a jack and a six. The dealer had a seven showing. Paulie stayed. The dealer flipped over his bottom card. A ten. Mandatory stay. Paulie sadly watched his chips being raked in.

A waitress walked by with a tray full of beers. Paulie didn't even notice her.


Apollo ran up the twisting fire escape that circled an old downtown hotel. It would have been grinding work anywhere, but in the stagnant heat of Las Vegas it was exhausting. The steps rang metallically under his feet. Each twist got him closer to the top. His progress spurred him on. The breath in his throat felt as hot as the air outside. He finally reached the top and leaned against the railing, panting, attempting to regain his breath.

Rocky stood at the bottom of the fire escape watching and waiting. Apollo looked down at him for approval.

"Again!" Rocky shouted.

"You slave driver!" Apollo rasped, but his voice was so weak Rocky couldn't even hear it.

Apollo started to run down the stairs. Rocky smiled. This was more like it.

\* \* \*

Back in the ballroom Apollo's hands were tightly wrapped inside the four-ounce gloves he had rejected earlier. Rocky held the heavy bag as Apollo punched it. The name, heavy bag, wasn't an exaggeration. The bag was the size of a bayonet dummy and weighed over eighty pounds. It could hurt a boxer if he didn't throw his punches correctly. It could damage the knuckles and cause shuddering shocks to run through the body. It was a stationary opponent, but still an opponent.

Apollo was throwing his punches steadily, alternating lefts and rights. He put all of his body into his punches, which gave them a concussive power. Rocky leaned against the bag, fighting to control it as it shook and shuddered with each punch. Rocky was used to this. In his younger days at Goldmill's Gym all the boxers took turns helping each other. It was like working with free weights. You needed somebody by you. As Apollo bore in, his fists hitting like hammers, Rocky felt he was holding onto a living, bucking thing.

"The right. Let the right go!" Rocky commanded.

Apollo let it go. Again. And again. Rocky was being buffeted like a ship at sea. The blows were causing indentations in the bag. Boom! Boom! Boom! The punches kept coming at the same steady pace. The blows were powerful enough to break bones.

"More. More. Give it to me. Show me what you've got!"

Apollo poured it on. He gave Rocky everything he had. The bag was beginning to hurt Rocky as it banged against him under Apollo's abrasive hammering.

But it was a sweet pain for Rocky.

Nighttime. The ballroom was deserted except for Rocky and Apollo. Apollo bobbed and weaved as he went through the lonely ritual of shadowboxing. He wasn't even wearing gloves, but his hands were wrapped. He continually took aim at an invisible opponent and punched away, connecting with air. Dance, swing. Dance, swing. Left-right combinations seemed to whistle in the still ballroom. An uppercut was followed by a powerhouse right.

"You're massacring him," Rocky encouraged.

Apollo put on a fierce scowl and started snapping his

punches so fast that they were hard to see.

"What kinds of boxers are there?"

"The quick and the dead!" Apollo snorted between punches.

"And what are you?"

"The quickest!" Apollo's shout boomed through the ballroom.

Dance, swing. Bob, weave. Jab, then fire the right. What a way to spend the night, fighting yourself in a deserted ballroom.

Unreal.


Paulie saw her sitting at the bar. She was gorgeous. Long blond hair framed a perfect face. Three-inch eyelashes didn't hide the glimmer in her eyes. She wore a skimpy dress that she had been poured into and was fighting to get out of. Her legs were crossed, revealing alabaster skin.

He was in love.

He forgot that he had just dropped most of his money at the crap table after spreading the bulk of his bundle at the slots and blackjack tables. He forgot that his main purpose was to help Rocky and Apollo. If he stayed dumbstruck where he was standing much longer he might forget his name.

He walked toward her, nervous but telling himself he had no reason to be. He was the champ's brother-in-law and Apollo's public relations man. A man with friends and influence. She might want a ticket to the fight. It was the hottest ticket in town. He could deliver that and more if given the chance.

He sat down beside her and cleared his throat. "Hello."

She looked him up and down and after a thoughtful pause decided to smile.

God, what a smile, Paulie thought.

"My name is Paulie."

She continued to smile, but now her eyes were sweeping the room.

"I'm Apollo Creed's public relations man."

"I'm in public relations, too." Her voice was everything he had hoped for.

"What a coincidence. Do you want a ticket to the fight?"

"No, thanks."

"What do you want?"

"A hundred dollars for an hour."

He should have known. He felt sad and stupid at the same time. Sad that she was a hooker and stupid that he hadn't left the crap table earlier when he still had a hundred. He knew that by the time he had found someone to borrow the money from she'd be gone.

"I'm the champ's brother-in-law. Can I get a discount?"

"If you were Rocky, it would be free. But you aren't, so beat it." She swiveled on her stool and turned her back to him.

Paulie walked away, humiliated and dejected. Maybe he and Las Vegas weren't made for each other.

Beat it. He wondered how she meant that.

Apollo was back jumping rope. As the date of the fight came closer more spectators showed up to watch his training. His feet pounded like Gene Krupa playing the drums. But now he wasn't bothering with crowd-pleasing tricks and gimmicks. D day was approaching and he was getting serious. But sometimes he couldn't help himself. You can be serious and have fun, too.

Rocky divided his attention between Apollo and the stopwatch. Suddenly a polka started blaring from the cassette player. Rocky almost jumped, he was so startled. Apollo collapsed in laughter, dropping the jump rope to the floor.

Rocky couldn't help himself. He started laughing, too.

Rocky and Apollo left the Grand dressed in sweat suits. The doorman looked at them, but didn't say anything. It was four in the morning and he had seen stranger sights at this hour.

They started jogging down the strip at a steady but not tiring pace. They passed Caesar's Palace, then Circus Circus. Before they knew it they were in downtown Las Vegas. It was lit up like high noon. It momentarily startled both of them. People thronged the sidewalks. Nobody paid the least bit of attention to them as they jogged by. Noises emanated from the casinos. It was obvious they were doing a rush hour business.

"Do you believe this?" Apollo asked.

"I gotta believe it, but I sure wouldn't want to pay the electric bill."

A giant neon cowboy waved at them from atop the Pioneer Casino. Rocky waved back without breaking stride. They passed Binion's Horseshoe Casino and jogged in place as they admired its display case of one million dollars cash—the last one hundred $10,000 bills in circulation in the country. Apollo whistled his appreciation.

They had to slow their stride because there were so many people on the sidewalks. They both wondered where the people came from, what a statistical readout on their homes, jobs, and incomes would look like. It seemed that every part of the country was represented among the nocturnal gamblers. Now they were passing quickie wedding parlors, escort services with signs in the windows announcing "It's legal in Las Vegas," and massage parlors that seemed more secretive about their services. But the main attraction was the people. They seemed to be everywhere and hurrying as if they were afraid they were going to miss something. The big jackpot, maybe.

"When do these people sleep?" Rocky asked, astonishment showing in his voice.

Apollo stifled a yawn. "More important, when do *we* sleep?"

The training continued. Rocky blew bubbles while Apollo exploded them with his lightning jabs. Rocky had confidence in Apollo's skill, but still he kept his eyes closed. He liked his teeth. They were very functional. He couldn't imagine being unable to eat corn on the cob for the rest of his life. He finally decided that the exercise could be dropped.

He had Apollo lay prone on a training table. Rocky started to pummel him in the midsection. It was like hitting wood.

Apollo laughed. "All those massage parlors in town and I end up with you."

"Funny, very funny," Rocky said as he let loose with an especially hard blow.

Apollo grunted his appreciation.

* * *

They were in their sweat suits again, but this time they weren't jogging. They were running sprints under the blazing desert sun. It was a trick Rocky had learned from Apollo in Los Angeles. Time and time again they raced each other. By the time the sun had started to go down they were both dead tired and had slowed to a walk.

"Long day," Apollo said, wiping sweat from his brow.

Rocky agreed. "How do you feel?"

Apollo smelled his armpits. "I could eat nails, Stallion."

"You look okay, but I think you need another week to sharpen up."

"No way. I'm ready now."

"Why don't we just postpone it a couple of weeks? Just a little insurance." It seemed reasonable to Rocky. The Russians wanted the fight so much he was sure that they'd agree.

"Can't do that." Apollo was emphatic.

Rocky hated it when Apollo got into a stubborn mood. His famous sense of humor would take long vacations when he wanted it to.

"Apollo, we don't know about this guy."

"He's a guy, that's all. A little bigger than some, but nothing special. Besides, what if I pull out and somebody else takes my place and whips him, where's that leave me?"

"What do you mean, 'leave you'?" Rocky asked, exasperated. "It's just an exhibition."

"That's where you're wrong!" Apollo stormed. "It's us against them."

Rocky wasn't sure he knew what Apollo was hollering about or even if it was for real.

"Do you always wanna be remembered as a guy who just took punches for money?" Apollo continued. "I don't. I wanna remember myself as somebody who did something. I gotta be more than this big-time champion watching the world go by. And if you don't understand what I'm talking about now, you will when it's over."

Rocky knew that he would find himself in Apollo's position someday. Life goes on, you get older, people notice you less. He thought he could cope with it, but he wouldn't know for sure until it happened. He felt tired, hot, and dirty. All he knew for sure was that if you say you're going to be in somebody's corner, you should be there all the way.

He put his hand on Apollo's shoulder. "Okay, let's give 'em hell."

They trudged back to the hotel leaving in the sand footprints that would soon blow away without a trace.

# Chapter 9

Ludmilla watched her husband as he did one-handed push-ups. She knew he could do them for hours. His strength never ceased to amaze her. *He* never ceased to amaze her. They had met while training for the 1980 Olympics in Moscow. Actually, the only difference between the Olympic training and the training that they did all the time was that instead of working in different cities the athletes had congregated in Moscow to get used to the city's climate. In Russia, being an athlete was a way of life. You didn't train for special events, you just trained. That was your job.

Their relationship was an attraction of opposites.

Ivan had been born in the slums of Moscow. His father was an alcoholic when he could afford to be. His jobs never lasted for more than a week. His mother sold tarts (commonly called twists) at the flea market. She officially received a hundred twists from the bakery every week, but she ended up selling two hundred. Ivan never did figure out where she got the extra hundred twists, but it taught him the necessity of working the angles—or, as they called it in Las Vegas, getting the edge. He soon started stealing, becoming a pickpocket and a burglar. It was lucrative and supplied the money that all adolescents lack. Soon he realized that the black market was an even more profitable venture. His first customers were Finns because of Finland's notorious dry laws. They periodically came to Moscow for binges. They went home hung over and broke. Ivan carried bottles of vodka and clothing that he had collected from garbage cans. He would trade with the drunken Finns for their vacation clothing. He was a quick learner (which would have been news to his teachers at school) and progressed up the ladder in the black market. There were firms (black market customers) for everything. He bought and traded foreign currency, sold illegal books, even passed counterfeit bills when he could find some to buy. His body grew along with his knowledge of the underworld. His success as a *fartsoushcik* (black marketeer) was soon insured because of his immense strength and physique. He didn't have to worry about disagreements with his competitors. He was beginning to acquire a reputation.

But then one of his boyhood friends was arrested for selling a copy of the novel *Lolita*. The official charge was distributing anti-Soviet material. He was sentenced under Article 58–10 of the Criminal Code to ten years at a labor camp in the Arkhangelsk province. Ivan started to reassess his life-style. He went to work at the Red Proletarian factory, but after a dispute with a superior who was a Party member he found himself working in the coal mines outside of Voroshilvograd. One day a film crew from the Moscow Film Institute came to the mines to make a documentary glorifying the proletarian worker. One look at Ivan Drago and they knew they had found their star. He looked magnificent begrimed with coal dust and sweat.

The film was seen by officials in Moscow and his potential as an athlete instantly recognized. He was quickly out of the mines and into a one-room apartment in Moscow, training under Manuel Vega to be a boxer.

Ludmilla still couldn't comprehend his background. She was born in Kiev. Her father was a Party official in charge of a beer bottling factory. They lived in a two-bedroom apartment and were envied by their neighbors. She couldn't remember learning to swim. It seemed to have come to her as naturally as breathing. At the age of eight she officially started training to be a world-class swimmer.

Ivan finished his push-ups and walked over to the table where his wife was sitting. He looked enviously at the bottle in front of her—it was Tuishi, a dry Georgian wine that had been favored by Stalin. The cold bottle was sweating in the dry desert air. So were they. But that's why Drago had come to Las Vegas to train—to get used to the climate. Neither of them understood why that was necessary when the fight was going to be held in a ballroom, but they both knew better than to question their superiors. It was the same old story of warriors and chiefs. She offered him her glass. Smiling, he refused and sat down by her. He leaned over and kissed her perspiring brow.

This was the side of Drago that the American Public hadn't seen. Ludmilla was the only thing he really cared about in the world. Meeting her had changed his life. Up until then he had cared only about himself. She had changed that. She had taken his anger and infused it with a gentleness that both pleased and alarmed him. He would do anything to protect her, to protect them.

They both knew what his orders for the fight were. There wasn't going to be any diplomacy in the ring. The victory was going to be more than decisive.

She hated to think of him going into the ring to maim another man deliberately. It was hard to reconcile with the gentle husband she went to bed with. But she also knew that he had no choice. He did what he was told and that was that. Questions would only bring trouble down on both of them.

He looked into her eyes and saw the pain. Her thoughts were obvious to him. He took her hand and held it against his cheek. She started to caress it lovingly, a brave smile forcing itself onto her lips. He closed his eyes, blocking out everything except the soft touch of her hand.

She knew what he meant. Forget Koloff. Forget Rimsky. Forget Creed. Forget everybody.

Except each other.

# Chapter 10

Adrian was finished packing her clothes. She was just taking one suitcase. Actually, it was more of an overnight bag than a suitcase. She was only going to Las Vegas for the fight. She and Rocky would leave the next day. Las Vegas had no appeal for her. She viewed it as a modern-day Sodom and Gomorrah, even though she knew those were two separate cities. Knowing Rocky, she was sure that the town had lost its attraction for him, too. Besides, even Paulie's friends who had been there said that three days was enough for anyone. Most of them had been broke after the first day. It wouldn't surprise her if the same thing had happened to Paulie. She loved him as a brother, but that didn't blind her to his shortcomings. In fact, sometimes he seemed to wear his failings like medals. Her wedding to Rocky had been as good for him as it was for her.

Rocky had been there a lot longer than three days. It seemed like three years, the way she missed him. It was the longest time they had spent apart since their marriage. It was like being separated from a part of your body or, even worse, a part of your mind. No, she didn't really mean that. Even when Rocky wasn't with her, she felt his presence. She sensed the sound of his footsteps in the hallway. Whenever she had gone into his study she imagined him seated at the computer, gamely struggling with an English program. His English sounded just fine to her. Beautiful. Just like Rocky.

She looked around the bedroom. The nights had been the hardest. She had become quite familiar with the late night programs on television. Johnny Carson and David Letterman had kept her company many evenings. She liked them, but they didn't compare to Rocky. And when she finally did go to bed she felt strange. The bed seemed so big that it was uncomfortable. She hadn't wanted to sleep without Rocky since that Thanksgiving years ago. It had started out disastrously. Paulie showed up drunk and tossed the turkey out the window. She and Rocky, in their mutual loneliness, fled to the skating rink where Rocky had shown a charming ineptitude that had embarrassed him. But then they had ridden the night trolley to Rocky's apartment on South Street and found happiness. He had taken her glasses off and told her she was beautiful. It had been like a Loretta Young movie she had once seen. Then he had kissed her and ended her loneliness.

Rocky Junior rushed into the bedroom. It seemed that he had forgotten how to walk. Lately everything was done at a run. It was funny when it wasn't driving her crazy. He slid to a halt.

"You all ready, Mom?" he asked.

Looking at him gave her pleasure. She knew he would resemble his father when he grew up. He was their creation. He wouldn't exist if it weren't for them. Pride and emotion welled up in her. She bent down and kissed his forehead.

"What's that for?" He felt that he was getting too grown up for that kind of display. What if one of his friends had seen it.

"Because I love you."

"Aw, Mom . . ." He squirmed under the attention, but it was a pretense. He loved her and thought she was the most beautiful woman in the world. But as you grew older, he felt, you had to react to certain things in ways that women didn't understand. He wasn't Mommy's little boy anymore. He didn't know what he was, but he wasn't that. He saw the suitcase on the bed and grabbed it. Light as it was, it almost pulled him to the floor. He manfully struggled with it until they were both upright and mobile.

He was happy that it had wheels on the bottom.

"You don't have to do that," she said, suppressing a smile.

"I want to."

He laboriously wheeled it out the bedroom door.

She wondered if he would like to have a brother. Or a sister. It was nothing definite; her period had been late before. But this time she had a feeling. Maybe she just wanted another baby to use as leverage to make Rocky retire. She hoped that wasn't so. A birth should be an event of awe and wonder, not manipulation. Well, she wasn't sure of anything yet, but it was a pleasant thought.

She went downstairs and gave Mrs. Tulio an endless list of last-minute instructions concerning everything from what part of the yard the gardener should work on to when Rocky Junior should go to sleep. The housekeeper wisely ignored her and went about her duties. Adrian smiled to herself. I must be getting nervous, she thought. Mrs. Tulio needed instructions about the house as much as Rocky needed boxing lessons.

She glanced at her watch. Cora had to come soon if they were going to get to the airport on time.

As if her thoughts had been read, the doorbell rang. It was Cora with the taxi driver standing behind her.

Adrian hugged Cora and greeted the driver, who took off his hat and nodded good morning.

The suitcase had managed to slow Rocky Junior down. By the time he got to the front door he was almost moving at a normal speed. It occurred to Adrian that it might not be a bad idea to permanently fasten weights to her son.

The taxi driver stepped forward. "Let me take that from you, young man." He pretended to struggle with the suitcase as if it were very heavy.

Rocky Junior beamed, knowing he had completed a man-sized job.

Adrian picked him up, held him tight, and kissed him.

"You be a good boy and do everything Mrs. Tulio tells you to."

"I will," he promised. Then, as if suddenly realizing that she actually wouldn't be home that night, he clung tightly to her, his eyes bright with moisture.

Adrian put him down. "You're going to be the man of the house."

That brightened him up a little. Cora kissed him and then they were gone.

Rocky Junior wiped the mist from his eyes as he watched the taxi drive into the street. Mrs. Tulio put her hands on his shoulders and guided him back inside the house.

Inside the cab Cora was silent, her eyes staring into nowhere. Adrian squeezed Cora's hand comfortingly. Cora came out of her private thoughts and smiled gratefully. Her face looked fatigued, worried.

"It's the plane," she lied bravely. "I always hate flying."

"Me, too," Adrian assured her.

"Not to worry," the driver chimed in. "More people die in car accidents than flying."

It was a comforting thought as they sped along the streets.

# Chapter 11

Fight night in Vegas: the biggest show in town.

The manager of Caesar's Palace stood outside his casino and glumly watched the crowds streaming into the MGM Grand. Who would have thought that an exhibition bout would cause so much commotion? Caesar's had become to boxing what Madison Square Garden once was. Several championship bouts had been held there. There was even a semipermanent 15,100-seat stadium in back by the tennis courts. Tonight it looked rickety and empty. He shook his head and went back into Caesar's. Who would have thought, he kept thinking, who would have thought? He wished he had a ticket.

The Grand had been booked solid for a week, which wasn't unusual, but the number of people that had to be turned away was extraordinary. Not even all the hotel guests had been able to get tickets, but they were satisfied just to be near the fight. So were many others. The parking lot was jammed. Ferraris were parked next to five-year-old station wagons. A closer inspection revealed a DeLorean or two.

Once inside the hotel the people encountered a gambling area that seemed to stretch as far as a couple of football fields. They were right—it was that large. The crowd inside was classic Vegas. Hollywood movie stars rubbed shoulders with midwestern conventioneers wearing name tags. But the casino was only a stopping point for the lucky ones with tickets. They continued to plunge toward the ballroom, which had a marquee over the main door that boldly proclaimed: SPECIAL EVENT—APOLLO CREED (U.S.A) VS. IVAN DRAGO (U.S.S.R.).

The inside of the ballroom was lined with bleachers— steel beams, pipes, and a lot of nuts and bolts hidden under velvet. Nobody seemed to mind. Pillows were hawked by vendors along with sundry wares. Wine and hard alcohol were spilled on more than one expensive outfit. Rock music pulsated from a live band's stereo equipment. Some of the people were dancing to the music, but it was difficult to keep from tripping over the cables that the media people had laid out. The entire scene had the aura of a fantastic but slightly decadent New York club. Skimpily dressed women sat on swings hung from the ceiling. Overhead a pair of small planes, one Russian, the other American, battled it out in a miniature dogfight. The sound was deafening. But even above that you could hear talking: the odds, who had the edge. The money game was going strong. Nobody seemed to care that it was just an exhibition match. In their minds it was the U.S.A. against the U.S.S.R. And Apollo had proved many times that he was one of the best the U.S. had.

The odds were two to one in Apollo's favor.

The ghost of Bugsy Siegel was doing business as usual, putting his money on the Russian, going against the odds.

It was quiet inside the Russian locker room. Everything that had to be done was done. Drago's hands had been wrapped, the gloves put on, the protective lubricant rubbed in where needed, his muscles massaged. He still reclined on the massage table, his eyes closed. It was impossible to tell if he was sleeping or thinking. Rimsky looked at his horizontal giant and smiled. He was the kind of fighter Rimsky had dreamed of—that all coaches dreamed of. In Rimsky's mind the fight was already over. Just another victory on the way to the world championship. He started folding a Russian flag. Manuel Vega and another Cuban were talking softly and gesticulating wildly.

Rimsky had never understood Vega, but now was not the time to try. He finished folding the flag. It would be used later, after Drago had demolished Creed. It was a nice thought.

Apollo was in high spirits. What had started as a whisper of a thought on a lazy afternoon was nearing fruition. His body felt ten years younger. He doubted he had ever been in better shape. Tomorrow the newspapers would be carrying pictures of him with his arms raised in victory. He'd be a national hero. Oh, sweet victory. Rocky continued to massage Apollo's shoulders even though there wasn't the slightest hint of tension in them. If Apollo was nervous, he wasn't showing it.

Rocky had picked up Adrian and Cora from the airport earlier in the day. He had missed Adrian, but he didn't realize how much until she had rushed into his arms. He didn't ever want to be separated from her for so long again. Cora had smiled and kissed his cheek, but the worry showed in her eyes. No matter what happened tonight, at least she'd be able to relax again. Rocky was glad of that.

Paulie was playing solitaire and losing. He wasn't surprised. When you're on a roll, you're on a roll, even if it's a bad one.

Duke paced up and down saying words of encouragement to Apollo, but in the back of his mind the image of Drago ran rampant.

The security guard knocked on the Russian's door. Rimsky opened it.

"It's time," the guard said, motioning for them to follow him.

The entourage filed out of the locker room with Rimsky in the lead. They were in the bowels of the hotel. The corridor they walked down was lined with security personnel, both Russian and American, and with various hotel officials. They descended a ramp and encountered a darkened boxing ring.

From the confused and bewildered looks on the Russians' faces, the hotel officials knew that a mistake had been made. One of the links in the chain of command had fouled up and the Russians hadn't been informed of the surprise entrance they were to make.

Rimsky looked at Drago. "What is this place?"

"I don't know," Drago answered in Russian. "Are we to fight here?"

An assistant manager of the hotel hurried up to Rimsky with an apologetic look on his face. This was going to cost somebody's job and he didn't want it to be his.

"I'm very sorry, Mr. Rimsky. It's obvious that there has been a communication failure here. It's perfectly okay. We just want you, as an ambassador of the Russian people, to make as spectacular an entrance as possible."

Rimsky didn't know what the hell the mousy little guy was talking about.

"It's show biz," the assistant manager further explained.

"What is this crazy place?" Rimsky demanded. "We fight in the basement like rats?"

The security guard held the ropes open. "Please get in and we'll go up," he explained, making an upward motion with his hand.

Now Rimsky understood. He didn't like it, but he understood. They were going to ride up in the ring like fools who couldn't walk on their own two feet. But he entered the ring, motioning for the others to follow him.

They all felt a sudden lurch.

"This is demented," Rimsky said.

The boxing ring started to ascend.

"Demented."

The crowd became silent as the floor in the center of the ballroom started to slide open. Even the band stopped abruptly. Nobody knew what was happening, but they all awaited with eager anticipation.

The boxing ring rose up through the opening in the floor. Everybody oohed and aahed. This was what they expected of Las Vegas. When they saw Drago a ripple of applause broke out. Rimsky was suddenly nervous. This was one of the strangest experiences he'd had in his whole career.

Drago looked out over the crowd, his eyes grave, his face impassive. The scene in front of him had to be a joke. They were making fun of him. Nobody fought in a place like this, not even Americans. His gaze softened as he saw Ludmilla seated at ringside. Koloff was in the chair beside her. Drago was grateful for that. There was no telling what these people were capable of doing. As his eyes continued to sweep the ballroom he became convinced that everyone here was deranged. That was the only explanation he could come up with. Everyone seemed to be staring at him. His eyes hardened as he glared back. He wasn't going to be played for a fool.

Hotel staff hurriedly set up tables and chairs around the ring. The reporters and Minicam operators were jammed around the ring. The television commentators, Halburn and White, settled into their chairs and immediately started talking.

"Welcome this evening to an unusual event," Halburn announced solemnly. "East finally meets West in professional sports. The Russian giant is already in the ring awaiting the arrival of the great former champion, the one and only Apollo Creed."

Drago and his ring men had moved to their corner. Rimsky took off Drago's robe and handed it to Vega. Drago started doing warm-up exercises.

"And maybe Drago has bitten off more than he can chew with Creed. He's dangerous no matter how old he is," White added.

Suddenly the band started playing again. It was a lively, raucous tune. A side door to the ballroom opened and a troupe of scantily dressed chorus girls holding small American flags entered. They were followed by Apollo with Rocky at his side. Behind them were Duke and Paulie. Apollo was dressed as Uncle Sam in a red, white, and blue suit complete with a top hat. The ballroom thundered with applause. Well-wishers tried to swamp the group as they made their way to the ring, but the polite, yet firm security men kept them at bay. Their job was made harder by Apollo. He kept reaching out to shake hands. When he reached the bandstand he jumped up and down in time to the music. The applause became so loud that the band itself was drowned out. Rocky shook his head in wonder. Who says you can't go home again? Apollo was doing it.

When they reached the ring, Duke held the ropes open and Apollo climbed in. Immediately he glared at Drago and started taunting him.

"I want you! I want you!" It was a familiar battle cry.

Apollo had used it many times, but he had never meant it so sincerely before.

Drago didn't even bother to look at Creed.

"Look at me! I might be the last person you see!"

The massive giant turned and stared blankly at Creed, his face immobile. Apollo might as well have been talking to himself.

"Save your energy," Rocky counseled as he handed Paulie Apollo's robe.

Cora was watching the show with mixed emotions. She was proud of her husband and pleased to see his obvious pleasure as he pranced around the ring. But her eyes kept returning to Drago. He looked like a mountain. Adrian reached over and gripped her hand. Cora was grateful.

"God, I feel born again," Apollo said joyfully to Rocky.

The tuxedoed ring announcer strode to the middle of the ring and motioned to the timekeeper, who rang the bell. The crowd became quietly restless.

"Ladies and gentlemen, welcome. Tonight's fight is being brought to you by Tiger Eye Promotions."

Apollo was bouncing around in his corner shadow-boxing, but his eyes were intent on Drago, and the furious jabs were directed toward him.

"Save some for the fight," Rocky joked.

"Thanks for getting me here, Stallion. I owe you."

"We're even."

The ring announcer continued: "Before we go any further, I would like to announce the presence of a true fighting champion who epitomizes the word courage—the Italian Stallion, Rocky Balboa!"

Waves of applause surged toward the ring.

Rocky smiled at Apollo and said, "Excuse me."

"Of course," Apollo replied, waving Rocky to the center of the ring like an usher.

Rocky walked around the ring waving at the cheering audience. They loved it. He was their champion and they showed it by applauding till their hands hurt.

The room was reverberating with so much noise that Halburn was having a hard time making himself heard.

"The great champion from Philadelphia is waving to his fans. He's not here to fight, but that doesn't matter to them. They're clapping loud enough to knock plaster from the walls. Balboa will be helping in Apollo's corner tonight. Apollo seems to be in fine spirits. He's definitely putting on a show for this capacity crowd."

"Balboa and Creed are truly an odd couple if there ever was one. Almost as odd as this location," White added.

"Definitely a first," Halburn agreed.

Rocky returned to Apollo's corner. The applause subsided.

"When do I get introduced?" Paulie asked.

"Tomorrow," Rocky answered.

Paulie was beginning to wonder why he had come on this trip. He had lost all his money and gotten his ego bruised by the women of Las Vegas. But on the plus side, he hadn't paid for the airplane ticket.

Apollo and Drago were glaring at each other across the ring. If the fight was going to be half as intense as the look they were giving each other, then it was going to be deadly.

The announcer gripped his microphone.

"Ladies and gentlemen, tonight's special event features two great athletes. In the blue corner, weighing 221 pounds, the former heavyweight champion of the world, the Dancing Destroyer, the Count of Monte Fisto, the King of Sting, the Happy Hitman—"

Rocky turned to Apollo. "Think you got enough nicknames?"

"We're almost done," Apollo said seriously.

The announcer's voice rose. "The Future Master of Disaster—"

"That's all of 'em." Apollo smiled.

"The one and only Apollo Creed!"

Apollo rushed to the center of the ring and jumped up and down, waving his hands in the air.

The crowd cheered wildly. The announcer once again held up his hands for silence, but he didn't get it. The cheers continued to thunder on. The announcer motioned to Apollo to go to his corner. Apollo did, and the crowd settled down a little, but the announcer still had to have the bell rung to get enough silence to be heard.

"In the red corner, weighing an even 261 pounds, gold medalist and undefeated world amateur champion from the Soviet Union, making his American boxing debut this evening—the Siberian Express, Ivan Drago!"

The applause was scattered and mixed with a smattering of boos.

Drago ignored the audience and continued to glare at Apollo.

Adrian had the curious feeling that someone was looking at her. She turned her head and saw Ludmilla, who was sitting a few seats away, staring at her and Cora. Ludmilla gave a friendly wave. Adrian smiled back at her. Encouraged by this response, Ludmilla got out of her seat and walked over to Adrian and Cora.

She shook hands with Adrian, then with Cora.

A photographer who had been forewarned by Koloff that this was going to happen snapped a series of pictures of Ludmilla being so gracious. The flash bar going off so unexpectedly startled Adrian and Cora, but Ludmilla was as poised as ever. She smiled stiffly at Cora.

"Good luck. I hope we can be friends."

Cora paused, then said, "I hope so, too."

Ludmilla turned to Adrian. "Nice meeting you."

Her job done, she hurried back to her seat. She felt relief sweep through her body as she sat down.

Koloff nodded to the photographer, who waved thanks back at him. He had some exclusive photographs. They were going to be happy back at his newspaper.

In the ring Rocky watched Apollo bounce on the balls of his feet.

"You okay?"

"Fine, Stallion, just fine," Apollo answered, his eyes still fixed on Drago.

"The bad blood between these two can be felt all the way in the last row—"

White interrupted his partner. "I can't get over the massiveness of the Russian."

"He certainly is a skyscraper," Halburn agreed.

The referee went to the center of the ring and motioned to the fighters to join him. Apollo was accompanied by Rocky and Paulie. The Russian contingent marched toward the referee in deadly silence. Drago's fierce, penetrating stare was still focused on Apollo.

The referee could feel the tension emanating from the two fighters. He felt he was standing between two jungle animals. He just didn't want to be the one that was chewed up and spat out. He was a professional, though, and kept his voice at a steady monotone.

"You both know the rules," he began.

Rimsky translated into Russian for Drago, who appeared oblivious to everything and everybody except Apollo.

"I want a clean fight. In the case of a knockdown, go to a neutral corner." A hint of nervousness crept into the referee's voice as he concluded, "Good luck to you both."

Just as Apollo was about to turn to go back to his corner, Drago said in clear English, "You will lose."

There was something about the matter-of-fact finality of the statement that rattled even Apollo. Drago continued to glare at Apollo as they returned to their corners.

Apollo shook his head at Rocky in wonder. "He's something else, isn't he?"

Rocky nodded agreement.

"Time to go to work," Apollo said, smiling. "I've got a few presents to give him."

"Specially gift wrapped, I hope," Paulie said.

Apollo's smile got bigger.

Duke leaned through the ropes and put Apollo's mouthpiece in. "Just don't get crazy. You're the man. You're the teacher."

"Yeah," Apollo grunted through the mouthpiece. "We're gonna do it, Stallion."

Rocky tapped Apollo reassuringly on the shoulder, then climbed out of the ring.

The bell rang. Round one.

Both fighters rushed to the center of the ring, eager to get at each other. Apollo wasted no time in slamming five blinding jabs into the Russian's static, stoic face. Drago didn't seem to notice them.

"Apollo appears to be in great form as he jabs sharply at the Russian. Drago slips that last combination with ease."

Drago was faster than anybody expected him to be. He moved around the ring confidently, not even attempting any real punches.

"The Soviet youngster is moving with surprising grace for a man his size," White commented.

Creed kept moving in, unleashing jabs and hooks as he took the fight to Drago.

"Creed on the attack again. The Russian smiles and slips away."

"Keep sticking," Rocky urged from the corner.

Apollo continued to pursue the elusive giant. This wasn't what he had expected, but he could work with it. He'd chase the Russian all the way to Siberia if it was necessary. Apollo changed direction and landed two swift jabs before Drago weaved away.

Koloff coldly watched the fight. Drago was following instructions. Everything was going according to plan. For once Koloff wasn't sweating. In fact the air-conditioning inside the ballroom was giving him a slight chill. It felt good. He felt good. He glanced at Ludmilla. Her eyes were focused intently on her husband.

Rimsky shouted out instructions in Russian. "Right hand over the jab. Do it!"

Apollo pressed forward, still connecting with his jabs, scoring points, but not damaging the Russian. Another solid job. *Wham.* Drago went over the jab with an express train right that exploded against Apollo's jaw. Apollo staggered. He began to backpedal, but it was too late. He had walked into the bear's cave and he was going to pay the price. Drago jumped forward, bombing Apollo with hooks and rights. Apollo was bobbing and weaving, but the blows were still coming through and taking their toll. Apollo was in trouble and he knew it. Just the blows landing on his arms were knocking him off balance.

"Oh, a crushing right by the Russian!" Halburn exclaimed.

"Creed is hurt!" White yelled pointlessly. Everybody watching the bout on television had already come to that conclusion.

The right hand had jarred Apollo down to his toes. He went into a protective crouch, his hands up successfully defending his head, but he was paying a high price as savage blows to the body rocked him back and forth.

Paulie watched incredulously. He had never seen anybody, even Rocky, handle Apollo like this.

Cora winced with each blow, trying but unable to close her eyes to the spectacle.

93

"Tie him up!" Rocky cried. "Hold him, Apollo. Grab him!"

Sensing blood, the crowd was roaring.

Duke couldn't believe what he was seeing.

Apollo attempted to grab the Russian and tie him up in a clinch to gain a few seconds to clear his head. Drago pushed him away effortlessly and shoved him into the ropes, but Apollo still managed to gain his few seconds. Drago cut loose with a thunderous hook. Apollo slipped it brilliantly. The Russian flew into the ropes from the momentum of his blow. Apollo backpedaled into the center of the ring and stood there waiting.

"Don't just stand there!" Rocky ordered.

Drago untangled himself from the ropes and moved toward Apollo.

"Move!" Duke screamed.

"The Soviet's strength is incredible! He just pushed Creed back as if he were a rag doll. No one was expecting this!"

Drago regained the center of the ring, his face still impassive. He was like a well-oiled machine.

Apollo lunged forward, unleashing a Sunday punch that began at his shoelaces. It exploded in the center of Drago's face. It barely slowed the Russian's momentum as he plowed forward for the kill.

"Do it! Do it!" Rimsky yelled. "Knock him out! Now!"

Vega quietly watched the fight, scrutinizing Drago's face to see if Apollo's right had done any damage. He didn't want a freak cut that would enable the referee to stop the fight.

Drago continued to connect. A right, a left, a short hook. Apollo went back to his crouch. An angry uppercut brought him out of it. Apollo went on valiantly counter-punching while trying to slip the Russian's devastating blows. He was managing to hold his ground, but why did he want to? Drago was loose, totally in control. His blows whistled in with a deadly grace. He didn't even grimace when an occasional blow of Apollo's connected.

"The Russian is hammering Creed. The punches can be heard in the tenth row," Halburn said, awe in his voice.

"But Creed isn't backing up. That's a big mistake. Why isn't he backing up?" White asked.

Apollo and the Russian were standing toe-to-toe, concentrating on trading punches rather than defending against them. Apollo was operating on guts instead of brains. He was going against everything he had taught Rocky. He wasn't the teacher anymore. He was raging flesh and blood going up against a cool, efficient machine. It was foolish, but he couldn't help himself. For every blow he landed, Drago landed three—and they were bone crunchers.

Ludmilla jumped to her feet, cheering for her husband. But then she looked at Adrian and Cora and sat down, subdued but still jubilant.

"Don't trade with him," Rocky yelled, exasperated. He knew what Apollo was doing and why; he had done it himself. You go against reason, against common sense. A voice deep inside you tells you that this is the only way to do it. The voice's name is pride.

"Is he crazy?" Paulie asked.

Yes, Rocky thought, we all are.

Apollo managed to step around Drago and drive an incredible flurry of picture perfect left-right combinations that momentarily halted the Russian. But instead of backing up for more punching room, Apollo insanely called for the Russian to come ahead. He yelled at Drago and gestured for the giant to come and get him.

The crowd roared its approval. This was the Apollo they knew and loved.

Enraged, and showing some emotion for the first time, Drago danced forward, feinted, stepped to the right, and smashed Apollo flush on the jaw with a powerhouse right that seemed to come from nowhere. Apollo felt his legs going. Feeling himself crumbling, he reached out and grabbed for the ropes. He slumped against them.

Drago moved in for the finish. Punishing body blows rocked Apollo against the ropes, but he didn't go down. The Russian was infuriated. He wanted this over with.

Everyone in Apollo's corner was shouting in unison. "Grab him! Tie him up!"

Apollo couldn't hear a thing. He was a sponge absorbing punches.

The bell rang. End of round one.

* * *

Apollo staggered over to his corner. Rocky and Duke rushed out to help him. They half supported him until he could sit down on the stool. He spat out his mouthpiece and slumped on the stool, his arms wrapped around the ring ropes. Duke started administering to a cut near Creed's left eye. Rocky wiped the blood from Apollo's nose while Paulie shot water into his mouth. Apollo seemed oblivious to all of them.

Drago strode confidently back to his corner and calmly sat down. Rimsky gave him forceful instructions in Russian, but Drago was staring intently at Ludmilla. She smiled at him. The expression in his eyes changed in a way that nobody but Ludmilla could detect. Rimsky shouted louder in his ear. Drago turned to him. It was time to get back to business.

Apollo's eyes were clearing, but his breath was ragged when it wasn't an out-and-out pant.

Duke looked with concern at the left eye. He had cleared the blood away and closed the cut, but the swelling around the eye kept increasing, almost to the point of closing it.

"Let's call it!" Duke said. "The fight's finished."

"Nothing is finished," Apollo retorted between gasps.

"You can't do no more, champ." Duke's voice was sad.

"I'm here to fight."

"He's killing you," Rocky said quietly. "I gotta stop this."

"Don't stop it! Promise you won't stop it. It's what I want!"

"Don't do this to me!" Rocky pleaded. But he knew it was useless. Mickey had begged him not to continue when he won the championship. He hadn't listened. Apollo wouldn't, either. Rocky didn't want to see his friend hurt, but he understood his desire not to stop. Rocky felt miserable. He wished he had listened to Adrian. "I don't wanna see you get damaged permanent."

"I got a right to get hurt," Apollo said, rising from the stool. "I'm doing it for me. Please. It's what I want."

"Okay," Rocky sighed.

The bell again. Round two.
Apollo didn't even make it to the center of the ring

before Drago was all over him. He wasn't boxing Apollo, he was mauling him. Granite-hard blows rained on Apollo. Every way Apollo moved he ran into a punch. The cut by the eye was open again with blood pouring out.

"Drago is all over Creed. He's going for the kill."

Cora was standing and screaming. She could hear every punch clearly. She had been hearing them in her nightmares ever since Apollo had left for Las Vegas. She hadn't known what the sounds were then, but she did now. They were hammer blows driving nails into a coffin.

"Stop this fight!" she shrieked. "For the love of God, stop it!"

Adrian grabbed her around the shoulders as Cora collapsed back into her chair.

Apollo was now being held up by the Russian, whose lethal, arching right hand smashed down again and again on the barely conscious Apollo. Drago looked at Apollo's bloody, battered face, paused, and looked at his own corner. Rimsky wildly gestured for him to continue the assault. Drago recommenced pounding away. All anger was gone from his face. He was expressionless. He could have been mining coal. His fist continued to strike like a pickax.

"Why they haven't stopped this fight is beyond me," Halburn said, shock in his voice.

Rocky had the towel in his hand and was on the verge of throwing it in the ring. Adrian rushed up to him.

"Rocky, he's dying," she exclaimed.

As Apollo slammed into the ropes he saw Rocky with the towel in his hand. He desperately shook his head no.

"My God, Creed wants to fight more." White couldn't believe what he was seeing.

Rocky looked at Duke.

"Throw it!" Duke yelled.

Rocky looked back to Apollo. The same desperate request was on Apollo's face. Don't do it. Don't throw in the towel on me. Don't quit on me.

Rocky dropped the towel to the floor. He couldn't deny Apollo.

In a final display of raw fighting instinct, Apollo rolled off the ropes and unleashed a flurry of jabs and hooks that managed to halt Drago's brutal assault. Even Drago was surprised.

The crowd went berserk. They were one hundred percent behind Creed.

The referee knew the fight should be stopped, but he also knew Creed was capable of miracles. Besides, he'd have the crowd all over him if he stopped it now.

"Creed has stung the giant! The Russian looks wild!"

"He hurt him!" Rocky yelled to Adrian. "He hurt him!"

Duke was hanging on the ropes. "Hook! Hook!"

Adrian looked at both of them in astonishment. Were they crazy? A man was committing suicide and they were cheering him on.

"Rocky, please stop this!" she shouted.

But all of Rocky's attention was on the ring. Apollo was still trying to battle it out with Drago in a face-to-face confrontation rather than use his boxing science. It was dumb and foolish and glorious. Apollo's punches began to falter, connecting with the impact of a pillow. Drago continued to land punch after punch, building to a sledge-hammer right that nearly decapitated Apollo.

Cora Creed ran to ringside, tears streaming down her cheeks. She grabbed Rocky by the arm.

"Stop it!" she cried hysterically. "He's killing him. Stop it!"

Rocky grabbed the towel and quickly threw it in the ring.

Drago was still punching. Apollo rocked savagely with each blow. It was amazing that he could still stand.

"The ex-champion is out on his feet. He's being pounded without mercy. Balboa has just thrown in the towel!" White yelled gratefully.

As soon as he saw the towel the referee stepped in and tried to separate the fighters. Drago paused again to look at his corner. Rimsky nodded grimly. Drago pushed the referee aside and delivered a final blow that could be heard over the din of the crowd.

"Drago is still attacking Creed. Somebody stop this!" Halburn was outraged. The boos from the crowd floated down like rolling thunder.

Apollo didn't know where he was. He felt lighter than air. He was flying and it was wonderful. All the could see were blurred lights of many different colors. He had never experienced anything like this before. He wanted to shout

98

how great he felt. Then he heard an explosion far, far away, and the many-colored lights shattered into blinding slivers of white that shot like rockets into a black field and disappeared, leaving only darkness.

The back of Apollo's head crashed into the mat with the sickening sound a watermelon made when dropped from a great height. The occipital lobe of Apollo's brain was crushed. Immediately hemorrhaging started. The blood swelled inside his cranial cavity, putting more and more pressure on the brain, literally squeezing it.

For a few seconds there was complete silence as everybody waited for Apollo to move.

Drago looked away as if he were no part of this incident.

Apollo was completely still.

Ludmilla lowered her head. When she looked up she saw Adrian glaring hostilely at her. The Russian woman looked around at the furious crowd and hurriedly made her exit.

Rocky and Duke jumped over the ropes and ran to Apollo. Paulie struggled through the ropes and followed them. Ringside physicians were squeezing through, medical bags in hand.

Koloff nodded dryly at Rimsky, who acknowledged the victory with a tight smile. Drago moved away from Apollo as if he weren't there.

"There's no movement by Creed! It's hard to see if he's conscious or not! It's absolute pandemonium!"

Rocky removed Apollo's bloodied mouthpiece. Reporters and cameramen had jammed into the ring, blocking the physicians.

Rocky looked at them furiously. "Let the doctors in here! Back up!"

Paulie and Duke roughly pushed them back. A Minicam fell to the mat with a loud crash.

The ring announcer stared at the frenzied activity in bewilderment. He looked at the timekeeper, who rang the bell.

"The winner by a knockout at fifty-two seconds of the second round, Ivan Drago." Then, almost to himself, he added, "What the hell's happening here?"

Cora slumped into a chair, crying hysterically. Adrian

99

hugged her, tears flowing down her cheeks, too.

The crowd roared its displeasure. It sounded and felt like an earthquake.

Rimsky took out his Russian flag, carefully unfolded it, and draped it over Drago's immense shoulders.

If possible, the boos and curses became louder.

Rimsky guided Drago to the center of the ring, took the microphone from the announcer, and handed it to Drago. Some of the cameras in the ring focused on the two Russians.

"My name is Drago. I cannot be defeated."

A stretcher had been brought up and Rocky was helping to put Apollo on it. The media personnel still crushed forward.

"Everybody get the hell back!" Paulie yelled, his face flushed with anger.

"Move it," Duke warned them, balling up his fists.

"Where's the ambulance?" Rocky asked.

"We've called for one," a doctor answered as he put his stethoscope to Apollo's heart.

"There's not one here?" Rocky couldn't believe it. Apollo was going to have a hell of a lawsuit against these people.

A Minicam operator slipped between Duke and Paulie and focused the glaring camera on Rocky. A reporter shoved a microphone in front of Duke.

"How is Apollo? Is he dead? How's Rocky taking this?"

"Get out of here!" Duke growled, fighting back tears as he looked at Apollo's inert body.

In the center of the ring the cameramen continued to film Drago as he droned his rehearsed speech.

"Tonight I fight an old man, an inferior American fighter."

Adrian and Rocky locked eyes for a terrible moment. The emotional turmoil the two shared crackled like electricity. Rocky turned back to Apollo and helped strap him onto the stretcher.

"Soon I defeat real champion and soon whole world will know my name: Drago!"

The cameras moved forward for close-ups of Drago. His face was unrelentingly fierce and grim.

Rocky held Apollo's face in his hands. It seemed odd to see him not flashing his big wide smile. It was as if he were sleeping, except that his breathing was becoming shallower, making a whistling sound.

"Where's the ambulance?" Rocky cried desperately.

No one answered.

A reporter queried Rimsky, "Did you ever think the fight would be so easy?"

"Yes. He was too old—very weak."

Rocky bent close to Apollo. He could still hear him breathing. Apollo was still fighting. He was never a quitter.

"Hold on, Apollo. You're strong. Hold on." Rocky said it like a chant. "Hold on. Hold on."

Another reporter questioned the victor. "Drago, Apollo Creed appears to be in very serious condition. Any comment?"

Drago looked at Rimsky.

"If he dies, he dies," Rimsky said solemnly.

Drago surveyed the confusion in the ring, his eyes blank and cold. He had done his job. He was content. Rimsky led him out of the ring. Security guards instantly surrounded them as the crowd surged forward, pelting the Russians with food and paper items. The Russian flag was stained by the time they reached the safety of their locker room.

With Drago and Rimsky gone all the reporters and cameramen turned their attention to Rocky and Apollo. There were too many for Duke and Paulie to contain.

"Get the hell back!" Paulie yelled as a cameraman got past him and started filming Apollo and Rocky.

Rocky turned into the camera'a glare. "Get that light off him!"

Duke grabbed the man by the belt and jerked him away from Rocky and Apollo. Rocky cradled Apollo's head in his arms.

"Hold on. You can do it. I know you can. Just hold on."

But Apollo let loose and flowed into legend.

# Chapter 12

*Amazing grace!*
*How sweet the sound*
*That saved a wretch like me!*
*I once was lost*
*But now am found,*
*Was blind*
*But now I see.*

The robed choir's ten voices rang clearly in the misty early morning air. It was a small funeral for such a flamboyant public figure. There were no more than thirty mourners at the graveside. Most of them were close friends or relatives, with the glaring exceptions of Koloff, Ludmilla, and their bodyguards. Shortly after their arrival a television film crew had appeared. Quite a coincidence.

Cora's black veil hid any tears that she might have been shedding. She stood up straight and proud, the way Apollo would have wanted her to. She knew that despite his public actions he had been a very private family man. Their two children stood beside her with brave but sad faces.

Rocky, Adrian, and Paulie stood on the other side of Cora. Adrian gripped Rocky's hand tightly. Paulie wore the same suit he had worn to Mickey's funeral.

After the fight there had been a barrage of newspaper

and magazine stories questioning the legality and morality of boxing. Despite the editorial stance of most that violence in the ring was to be deplored and condemned, they all highlighted grisly photos of Apollo's death. Letters to the editors of various newspapers had suggested that retaliatory steps be taken against Drago—an eye for an eye, a boxer for a boxer. Of course, none of these courageous letters was signed.

The casket was simple: black with brass handles. Under the closed lid Apollo reposed on white satin.

Rocky stared at the casket, so lost in his self-condemnation that he barely heard Duke's eulogy.

"Men are made for the end from the very beginning. Apollo Creed was a warrior. He lived and he died by the code of the warrior. The warrior has the right to choose his way of life and his way of death, and we are bound to respect this sacred right."

Cora knew that Duke meant well. He had been Apollo's friend from the very beginning. They were almost like brothers. But she couldn't agree with a philosophy that condoned what had happened. She didn't want her sons to grow up to be boxers. Years back there had been a national outcry of rage after a woman in New York had been stabbed to death while her neighbors watched without attempting to intervene. But thousands had been cheering while Cora's husband was beaten to death in Las Vegas. She had more respect for the people in New York who had closed their doors to the poor woman. At least they had had enough sense to know that something was wrong and that they should be afraid. But people had paid to see her husband murdered. She could think of no other word for it—it was murder, just as surely as if he had been stabbed to death. No, she didn't want her sons to be warriors. She wanted them to be men.

"He knew that with all his success he had not come close to answering the questions he had inside. And he pushed hard to find those answers. Now only he knows whether he found them. His place among those who loved him will be empty until one day it is filled and the circle is completed. Thank God men are made for the glorious end in the beginning."

Adrian looked at Rocky. His reddened eyes were set in a dark look of vengeance. It upset her. He had been this way since that night—the night Apollo died because he couldn't give up boxing. The implications of that thought terrified her.

Rocky stepped forward and put his heavyweight championship belt on the casket. The television crew moved in closer to get a better shot.

Koloff nodded to Ludmilla. She stepped forward and approach Cora, a folded American flag in her hands. Koloff followed her. The director of the film crew indicated to the cameraman to focus on the Russians and Cora.

Koloff spoke first.

"Excuse us, we are very sorry over your tragic loss. Ludmilla wanted to show our respect."

"Move in closer," the director whispered to the cameraman.

"I feel the pain as much as you," Ludmilla said softly. "But we are both wives of fighters. No one is to blame."

"No one?" Cora asked, irony crackling in her voice. Apollo hadn't beaten himself to death. There had been two people in the ring that night.

"It is the life we choose to live. Your husband was a good man."

"How do you know what he was?"

"Because you are a good woman. Please take this as a symbol of friendship and respect."

Cora stared at the flag, then back at Ludmilla.

"We brought our own," she said dryly.

Cora motioned to her oldest son. He stepped forward and placed an American flag next to Rocky's belt on the casket.

"Please," Ludmilla went on, faltering, "accept my sincere sympathy."

Cora didn't answer. Instead she nodded to Duke, who motioned to the cemetery man. There was a whirring noise, and the casket began its descent.

Ludmilla and Koloff hurried off, their security men hustling after them.

Rocky stared at Cora. She looked back at him, her gaze hard and steady.

"He was your friend...."

Rocky felt a chill go through him.

"Why didn't you stop it?" Cora demanded.

Rocky lowered his eyes to the casket. He had no answer.

The casket hit the bottom of the grave with a dull clunk.

Cora took her children and left. The other mourners departed, too.

"See you, Apollo," Paulie said, and, taking Adrian by the arm, he walked to the waiting limousine.

Rocky took one last look at the grave, then joined them.

Rocky gazed out the tinted window of the limousine. He looked miserable, maybe even worse than when Mickey had died.

"I know what you're thinking." Adrian broke into his thoughts. "You want revenge. Don't let this happen. You can't do anything for Apollo now. What if you end up the same way? Apollo wouldn't want that. It could happen, you know. You're not Superman, you're just a man. Boxing has already killed your two best friends."

Paulie didn't take offense. He knew what she meant.

"You said before you were afraid of losing everything, Rocky. You might do it if you keep thinking like this."

"I let it happen," Rocky said bitterly.

"No, you didn't. It was no one's fault. You can't take all the blame. He was your friend. You would have done anything to protect him. You have to believe that. You do believe that, don't you?"

Rocky continued to stare out the window, his eyes distant, his jaw tense. Adrian watched him, feeling helpless.

Paulie could feel the tension emanating from Rocky. Something was going to happen.

# Chapter 13

Rocky pulled the car over to the curb of the busy New York City street and parked, leaving the motor idling in neutral and pulling up the emergency brake. Paulie got out of the passenger side and walked around the front of the car. A policeman scrutinized him carefully. The black sports car was parked in a red zone. When Rocky got out the policeman recognized him and waved. You didn't give a ticket to the champ. Rocky waved back as he held the door open for Paulie. Paulie slid in behind the steering wheel, a delighted smile filling his face. He felt like a kid again. Rocky leaned down by the window.

"I want you to park this and wait for me in the coffee shop on the first floor. Got it?" Rocky asked.

"Got it!" Paulie assured him, too enthusiastically.

"I don't wanna see no dents in this when we go home."

Paulie's face assumed a look of violated innocence. How could Rocky even think that? Rocky pushed the lock button down on the driver's door and stepped away from the car. Paulie eased the car into the traffic without signaling.

Rocky frowned, then stepped onto the sidewalk. Newspapers hung from a kiosk on the corner, their headlines still branding Drago a monster. The story was as hot as ever. Busy city humanity surged around him. Some gave him curious stares, but most of them were too involved in their own problems to even notice him. Besides, he was dressed in a business suit, not boxing trunks. He stared up at the monolith in front of him. It was an older skyscraper, more concrete and steel than glass.

Rocky's gaze lingered on the thirteenth floor. The United Boxing Federation was located there. Rocky had a meeting scheduled with them today. He had sent them a proposal and now he was going to hear their reply. He took a deep breath and entered the building.

The five-man commission and the Federation lawyer all sat on one side of the long, polished conference table; Rocky sat on the other. The commissioners looked alike, sounded alike, even dressed alike. Rocky felt he was addressing a body with five heads. He didn't like what the five heads were saying, and his displeasure was obvious. The lawyer looked sympathetic, but Rocky knew that meant nothing. A lawyer was a lawyer was a lawyer. The atmosphere of the room was tense.

"We've gone over the facts many times, Mr. Balboa, but the answer is still the same."

Rocky shifted in his chair. He was tired, despondent. His haggard face showed that he hadn't been sleeping well. Nothing had gone well with him since the Creed fight.

"Can't you change the rules?" he asked.

"Under the present Federation rules, a fight between you and this Russian is not and will not be permitted."

Rocky stared coldly at them. The Spanish Inquisition had had rules, but that didn't make it a good thing. Rules didn't exist by themselves. They had to be made by people, interpreted by people, and changed by people.

"Let's be realistic," one of the commissioners said more informally. "The Russian has yet to have one legitimate professional fight. His bout with Creed was a publicity stunt that backfired. Whether you want to believe it or not, Drago is still considered an amateur."

They obviously hadn't seen Drago fight, Rocky thought. If the Russian was an amateur, then Xaviera Hollander was a virgin.

"It's unfortunate that these things happen," the commissioner continued, "but they do."

"The bout with Creed was just a fluke," another one of the heads added.

A fluke! Rocky gripped the arms of his chair tightly. He could still see Apollo's head smashing into the mat. A dead man is not a fluke. He's a dead *man*!

The car's motor purred a lullaby to Paulie as he drove along the crowded streets. He had meant to go straight to a parking lot, but once he started gliding along in the sports car his iron will melted. He pushed a button and the window slid down. The street noises rushed in, vitalizing him even more.

Before he knew it he was in Times Square, drawn to it like iron filings to a magnet. He gawked out the window. What a circus. People were strutting up and down Forty-second Street in some of the most outlandish outfits he had ever seen: leather mixed with lace, steel chains with velvet gloves. Prostitutes, pimps, bums, tourists, even New Yorkers lined the sidewalks. When Paulie wasn't leering he was laughing. It was all so sordid and silly. Maybe not *that* silly. He was glad that he was in the car, a spectator, not a participant.

Suddenly a taxi lurched out in front of him. Paulie slammed on the brakes, almost driving his head through the windshield. He was fast, but not fast enough. Slam! He heard the sickening crunch of metal against metal. The burly taxi driver got out of his car with an angry scowl on his face and four-letter words rushing from his mouth like a raging river.

Paulie slumped down in his seat.

Why me, Lord, why me?

"Let's be rational. Once Drago moves up in the rankings—once he is in the top ten—you have our blessings."

"That might take a couple of years," Rocky said, his voice weary.

"Yes, it could. But if it helps prevent another fatality, it's well worth it."

But what about the fatalities Drago might cause while working his way up the ranks, Rocky wondered.

The lawyer leaned forward earnestly. "The best way to have boxing banned is to have one more accident—"

"Especially of this magnitude," interjected a head that had previously been silent.

The lawyer frowned at him, then continued. "The public harassment and legal entanglements would be extraordinary."

Rocky didn't have to put his foot into something to know what it was. Sugarcoated or not, it smelled the same. The world might be a lot better off if people kept their good intentions concerning other people to themselves.

"What you're really saying is you don't think I have a chance, right?" Rocky demanded.

The commissioner's smile was condescending. "What we're saying is why tempt fate. Let's find out more about this man. Let's see what develops. So far, he's had one professional fight, and one man is dead."

Rocky shook his head in disgust. You're really telling me news, he thought as he rose from his chair and strode angrily towards the door.

"Rocky, I'm sure you want to know the bottom line on all this," the lawyer said earnestly. "It's all rules. You have rules, we have rules, and everyone has to abide by those rules. It's that simple."

Rocky knew there wasn't a damned thing in this complex world that was simple. He paused, the door half-open.

"There's gotta be a time when rules stop and people start."

The door slammed shut on Rocky's eloquent last statement to the commissioners.

Paulie wasn't in the coffee shop and there was still food on the shelves. Unusual, Rocky mused. He stepped out onto the sidewalk and abruptly stopped. Paulie was standing by the right front fender of the car, but even his girth couldn't hide the huge dent. Rocky groaned.

"Rocky, I can—"

The words started to rush out of Paulie's mouth. Rocky sighed.

The end to a perfect day.

# Chapter 14

Adrian had told Rocky about her pregnancy before he submitted his request to the United Boxing Federation. He was happy, but it didn't change his decision to fight Drago. She didn't understand, and he couldn't explain it to her. It was just something that he had to do. Needless to say, their relationship became strained. They talked less and less, and Rocky thought he saw an accusatory look on Adrian's face. Rocky Junior sensed that something was wrong, but he was used to not understanding things, so he took it in stride. Adults could learn a lot from kids, he thought.

The decision of the Federation disappointed Rocky, but it didn't deter him. He had put his championship belt on Apollo's casket; now he handed the title back to the Federation. If he couldn't fight on their terms, then he'd fight on his own—or, as it turned out, on the Russians'.

The press conference had been hastily called, but that didn't affect the attendance of the media personnel. The banquet room where the conference was being held was packed with reporters, Minicams, and still photographers. The glare from flash bars and Minicams was intense. Attention was focused on a long table at the front of the room. Rocky and Paulie sat at one end of the table; the Russian contingent, including Ludmilla, sat at the other.

There was none of the ballyhoo or sense of show biz that had characterized the previous press conferences. No jokes, no smiles, just questions and answers.

"Rocky, is the decision final?"

"Yes."

"Rocky—Rocky, over here, please," another reporter called. "Is this the first time a champion has given up his crown?"

"That I don't know."

"Doesn't the title mean anything to you anymore?"

"Not until this is over," Rocky answered with a hardness in his voice that surprised even Paulie.

The attention shifted to the Russian side of the table.

"We know you've agreed to take this fight. Do you think you're moving along too quickly?"

"Why wait?" Rimsky said. "Drago is ready now."

"But Rocky Balboa will have no official championship title. If you win, it will be a hollow victory."

Koloff scoffed at the statement. "The world knows he is the true champion. When he is defeated we will be recognized as the best in the world."

"Drago?" A reporter waved for recognition. Drago nodded his head. "Any feelings on this fight?"

Whispering, Koloff translated the question to Drago and listened to his reply. He smiled broadly at the press.

"Drago has told me it will be an easy fight."

Ludmilla looked at Koloff suspiciously. She wondered what Drago had really said.

"Coach Rimsky, considering Rocky's known punching power, do you think this fight will be easy?"

Rimsky glanced at Koloff, an uneasy look of hesitancy in his eyes. But Koloff nodded firmly. Rimsky's voice was a flat monotone as he replied, "Yes, of course. As easy as the fight in Las Vegas."

A grim silence greeted this statement.

Rocky glared at Rimsky.

Koloff broke the silence. "It is a matter of science and evolution, isn't it, gentlemen? Drago is thirteen years younger and the most perfectly trained fighter ever. This other man has not the size or the stamina or the genetics to win." He looked over at Rocky and laughed. "It is physically impossible for this little man to win. Drago is a look at the future."

A reporter glanced questioningly at Rocky.

"What do you say to all this?"

"I'll do my talking in the ring."

"Rocky, there's no mention of it so far, but what's your salary for this fight?"

"No money."

Astonishment. "Nothing?"

"It's not about money."

This was a different Rocky than the reporters had seen before. He seemed older, harder.

"Has the fight date been set?"

"In nine weeks, December twenty-fifth."

"On Christmas? Why Christmas?"

"That's the day I was told," Rocky said.

Paulie looked at Rocky in disbelief. Rocky had been acting strangely since Apollo's death, but he had done nothing to indicate that he was this irregular. Nobody fights on Christmas day. There was something eerie about it.

"Are you nuts?" Paulie whispered discreetly.

"Rocky, what's going on here?" somebody asked, confusion evident in his voice.

Instead of replying, Rocky just stared at Drago, his eyes glistening like dark marbles.

"There's a rumor that the fight's going to be in the Soviet Union—Leningrad, to be exact. Is that true?"

"Yes," Rocky confirmed.

Jeez, first Christmas day, now Leningrad. Paulie wondered what was coming next. Pistols at fifty paces, maybe. Paulie didn't even have a winter coat. He had spent all his money getting the fender repaired. Rocky hadn't wanted him to, but Paulie had insisted, at Adrian's urging. He wondered how the beer was in Russia.

"Why did you agree to this?"

"I'll go where I have to go."

The reporters thought that Rocky was making Clint Eastwood seem like a real blabbermouth.

"We fight in Soviet Union or we fight nowhere," Koloff said. "Why don't you ask his wife why. Ask why she is afraid of what will happen here." He looked at Ludmilla. "Tell them, please."

Ludmilla didn't need much urging. "I am afraid for my husband's life. We have threats of violence everywhere."

"There is not only the violence in this country. There is the fact that we would never get a fight judged fairly here. Yes, we fight in Soviet Union or nowhere," Koloff concluded.

"Why the sudden change in attitude towards America?" a reporter asked, remembering the previous speeches Ludmilla had made.

"No, you changed, not us," Ludmilla said, her voice rising in pitch. "We came here as visiting athletes, not as enemies, but you call Drago a murderer. No, you changed, not us."

A reporter jumped on that. "Are you making a political statement with this fight?"

"We are not in politics," Ludmilla insisted. "All I want is for my husband to be safe, to be treated fairly."

"What makes you say he isn't being treated fairly?"

"You—the press! You call him a *killer*! He's a professional fighter, not a killer. You have this belief that you are better than us. You have this belief that this country is so very good, and we are so very bad—that you are so very fair, and we are so very cruel."

"Yes," Koloff added, "these are all lies and false propaganda to support this antagonistic and violent government."

Paulie jumped to his feet. Enough was enough.

"Violent? We don't have to keep our people in with no wall or machine guns!"

"Who are you?" Koloff demanded.

"Who am I? I'm the unsilent majority, big mouth!" Paulie shouted.

"Yes, insult us. It's more typically rude behavior toward foreign visitors." Koloff's smile wasn't pleasant. "Well, perhaps the simple defeat of this little so-called champion will be a perfect example of how pathetically weak your society has become! We go now."

The Russians stood up and started to walk out. As Drago passed Rocky he stopped and glared down at him. Rocky got to his feet and silently returned the stare.

"For you, I feel one thing," the Russian giant said in clear English, "pity."

Flash bars went off like firecrackers as photographers rushed forward, pushing each other as they tried to get a better angle of this classic confrontation.

"I can read the headline now," a reporter joked. "'Grudge Fight Set for Soviet Union.'"

It was on the front page of the sports section the next morning.

# Chapter 15

The Russians departed for their homeland as quickly and quietly as a secret diplomatic pouch. It was assumed that they were no longer interested in becoming acclimatized to America. Besides, they had accomplished their original mission. Drago was going to have his bout with Rocky. Even better, the fight was being held in Russia, more than Koloff had hoped for! His superiors were so happy with him that a close examination of his methods had been curtailed. The end justified the means. As Koloff punned: the road to Utopia could be rocky.

The mayor of Philadelphia sent in a maintenance crew to restore Goldmill's Gym, and within a matter of days it was in condition for Rocky to train in. Rocky thanked the mayor, explaining that he was grateful for a familiar, quiet place in which to work out. But it wasn't that way. When Rocky arrived at the gym with his training bag in his hand and Paulie by his side he discovered that the reopening of the gym had been turned into a gala publicity affair. It was the same old thing again: aggressive photographers, blinding Minicams, friendly but probing reporters.

A large flag was strung across the center of the gym, and many of those present waved small American flags. Paulie wished he had thought of that gimmick. There was money to be made here. Others carried placards with various slogans printed on them: AMERICA #1, DON'T BOMB—SEND ROCKY, BEAT THE BEAR, PRIDE OF AMERICA, U.S.A. ALL THE WAY.

Duke stepped out of the crowd. "Hey, Rock. Great to see you."

"Thanks," Rocky said as they shook hands. "What is this?"

"Looks like you got people crazy around here."

Rocky recognized a lot of familiar neighborhood faces in the crowd. Father Carmine hadn't changed a bit. Mike, the old cleanup man at the gym, now shuffled instead of walked, his gray flattop hairstyle replaced by a bald pate ringed with snow-white hair. Joe Czack looked too heavy to get behind the bar he tended, much less to climb through the ropes of a ring. Spider Rice was as shy and hesitant as ever and his smile was just as warm. The Big Dipper was shrinking with age, but his handshake was still firm. Some were noticeable by their absence. Tony Gazzo, Rocky's former employer, had retired from the loan-sharking business when somebody put a bullet in his head. His ever-present bodyguard, who resembled a glum cigar store Indian, had died from grief at the same time with two bullets in his head. Others were just missing—frozen under a pile of papers in an alleyway, lost on a barstool. Life went on.

A button-down-type sportscaster from one of the local television stations jammed a microphone in front of Rocky.

"Rocky, can we have a quick word with you?"

"I really don't have a lot of time. I'm here to work."

"Just a few minutes, please," the sportscaster begged.

Rocky reluctantly gave his okay.

The sportscaster turned to his crew. "Roll," he commanded, looking into the camera. "We're here for what appears to be a pep rally, but in truth it is a gathering of fight fans and well-wishers for Rocky Balboa. The reason? Today he starts training for the Russian giant, Ivan Drago." The sportscaster directed his attention back to Rocky. "Rocky, you're back in the gym preparing to defend a title you no longer possess. Why?"

"What's just the way things worked out."

"There have been rumors that you peaked after you defeated Clubber Lang and that you're ready to be taken."

116

Paulie took umbrage at that. "That's a stupid question. Refuse comment, Rocko."

"There's always a chance of losing, but it's how you lose that counts," Rocky said quietly.

"Though the Russian is relatively unknown, the odds are even at this point. How do you feel about this lack of confidence from the fight authorities?"

"That's how it is."

"Today's sports section stated that you, thirty-eight years old with aging legs and over seventy-five hard professional fights behind you, should perhaps have retired—and now, with this fight being set on Christmas day, the whole event is being called 'The Immaculate Deception'. Any feelings about it?"

Rocky smiled at Paulie.

"Y'know, Paulie, it's funny how the same guys that worked hard building you up work harder tearing you down."

Both Paulie and Duke nodded grim agreement.

Rocky turned back to the sportscaster. "Thanks for coming over, but I gotta go now."

"One last thing," the sportscaster persisted. "Don't take this wrong, but what is the real reason for fighting the Russian? For the glory or the guilt?"

"Guilt?"

"For what you let happen to Apollo Creed."

The brash young sportscaster wilted under Rocky's penetrating stare. He knew he'd have to change shirts after this interview.

"You're pushing real hard," Rocky said. "I hope you get a raise."

The sportscaster let out a sigh of relief.

Bedtime for a little boy.

Rocky slung his son Tarzan-style over his shoulder and carried him up the stairs. Rocky smiled as the padded feet of the pajamas squirmed in front of him.

"It's still early," Rocky Junior said, his voice muffled by Rocky's back.

"No, it isn't."

"I don't want to go to sleep."

"How're you going to grow?"

"Take vitamins."

The kid was quick. Rocky gave him credit for that.

"Wise guy." He thumped him affectionately on his rear.

"Daddy, everybody says you've gonna fight a giant man."

"Yeah, he's tall."

"Why?"

"Because he took his vitamins," Rocky joked.

"That's not what I mean."

"It's something I've got to do," Rocky said soberly.

They entered Rocky Junior's bedroom. A single lamp was on by the bed. Its glow revealed an array of neatly placed toys. Mrs. Tulio had been hard at work trying to make order out of chaos. Good for her, Rocky thought, it's the effort that counts. He lowered his son to the bed and pulled the covers over him.

"Dad, the kids at school say you're gonna lose. They think you're getting too old to fight."

"I am, believe me."

"I want to fight, too."

"No way!" Rocky said firmly.

"Why not? You do it."

"I do it 'cause I have to. I do it so you won't have to. Understand?"

"No."

"You will. I want you to use your head, not your hands, to make a living. That's what would make me proud."

Rocky bent over and kissed his son. Rocky Junior hugged him tightly. Rocky turned out the lamp and started for the door.

"Daddy?"

"Yeah?"

"I think you'll win."

"I love you," Rocky said.

"I love you, too." It was a beautiful voice floating out of the darkness.

Rocky closed the door behind him and stepped out into the hallway. Adrian was at the bottom of the staircase. They locked eyes for a fleeting moment, then almost painfully stepped out of each other's view.

Rocky was tired from the day's workout. He let Paulie drive the car. Paulie saw it as a promotion of sorts. As they approached the driveway a group of women of various ages wearing red, white, and blue ribbons on their coats surrounded the car. Rocky sighed and lowered his window. The smiling faces bunched together by his door. The group leader handed him a folded flag.

"Mr. Balboa, we hope we're not disturbing you, but we represent the Sisters of the Revolution, a group that upholds the American ideals. And we would like to present you with an American flag that has actually flown over the Capitol."

"Thank you," Rocky said, resting the flag on his lap.

"You're welcome," the woman beamed, "and you're an inspiration to us all."

"Thank you."

"Hope you knock him out." The statement sounded odd coming out of her grandmotherly mouth.

Rocky smiled and nodded his head reassuringly.

Paulie pushed the gate beeper and proceeded down the driveway. Before the gate closed Paulie caught a glimpse in the rearview mirror of the women still waving.

"Don't let it bother you," he told Rocky, "they mean well."

"Don't we all," Rocky mumbled.


Rocky noticed a strange car parked by the garage. It was one of those supposedly anonymous-looking cars that screamed *official business*. Rocky's only question was whether it was local or bigger than that.

Rocky and Paulie entered through the kitchen door. Rocky Junior was making a colorful concoction in a dripping salad bowl. It would be either delicious or toxic.

"Hi, Dad."

"Hi, what're you doing?"

"Making Jell-O."

Paulie thought that maybe he'd call out for pizza for dinner.

"Nice color," Rocky commented. "Don't you wish you could swim in something like that?"

"Oh, that's weird!" his son squealed appreciatively.

Adrian entered, her face softer than Rocky expected.

"I'm glad you're home," she said, kissing him on the cheek. "We have company."

"I saw the car. Who?"

"Two men from the State Department."

Rocky took Adrian by the hand and they left the kitchen.

Paulie took a closer look at his nephew's masterpiece. Maybe it could be saved yet.

"Add some bananas and don't ask no questions."

The two State Department men were sitting on the couch, coffee cups in hand, when Rocky and Adrian entered the living room. They were both in their forties, one a little thicker around the waist than the other. Both were dressed in conservative business suits and the same color ties. Tweedledee and Tweedledum. They put down their coffee cups and rose as Rocky crossed the room. Adrian made the introductions.

"Rocky, this is Mr. Griffin and Mr. Holmes."

Rocky shook hands with both of them.

"Pleasure, Mr. Balboa," Griffin said. "I'm a big fan of yours."

"We both are," Holmes confirmed.

"Beautiful home here," Griffin said, waiting for a reaction from Rocky as to how their visit was affecting him. Was he curious? Intimidated? What?

Rocky just nodded.

"Well, you're a busy man," Griffin continued, "so we'll get down to the reason we're here."

At this point Paulie entered with a half-devoured Yankee Doodle creme-filled abomination in his hand. The robot trailed behind him carrying a beer.

The government men were startled by his and the robot's appearance.

Paulie held up the Yankee Doodle.

"Yo, Adrian, weren't there two of these left?"

"You had one for breakfast."

"I had eggs and bacon."

"Eggs, bacon, and a Yankee Doodle," Adrian reminded him.

"Oh," he said, disappointed. But then one was better than none.

Rocky looked at the visitors. "You were getting to the point...."

"Aptly put," Holmes said. "The State Department has been following the details of this fight for quite a while, and, quite simply, we have been asked to request that you not go to Russia and take part in a fight of this magnitude under these circumstances. We believe that this type of contest—you know, the typical us against them—can only cause the two countries to move further apart and create further friction in relations." He smiled nervously. "Already people are calling it World War III."

"I know what you're saying," Rocky said.

"Of course you do," Griffin agreed. "The controversy is only going to grow, the national fervor is only going to grow, and if something very unfortunate were to happen—"

"Like if you lose—" Holmes interjected.

Griffin was surprised by his associate's bluntness. He tried to smooth it over. "It could happen."

Holmes plowed on. "And with it would come tremendous international embarrassment, and truthfully, at this stage of your career, you don't need unnecessary embarrassment and humiliation, and neither does your country."

Now it was Griffin's turn to be blunt. "Of all the data we've reviewed, along with the extensive computer readouts, it is conclusive that you're going to lose. I mean, Mr. Balboa, let's face it, you can't beat the computer."

"Never fought one," Rocky said calmly. "Y'know, all I want to do is settle something for me. I don't want to embarrass this country or anybody else. I love this country, it gave me everything I got. But this fight is about punching, not politics. It's just between two men."

"It's more involved than that," Holmes assured everyone.

"No, it isn't," Adrian declared. "Like he said, this is just between Rocky and another man, no politics, no grandstanding. He's given up his peace of mind, and," she added, looking pointedly at Rocky, "he seems ready to give up anything to do this. And you have no right to stop him, no matter what you think."

"We can revoke your passport," Holmes threatened.

Adrian strode angrily from the room. Rocky watched her, his eyes shining with pride. She was a real clutch hitter.

Paulie grabbed the beer from the robot and took a king-size swig.

"He ain't doing nothing illegal so you ain't revoking nothing. And you ain't dealing with morons here. You guys are federal employees and we're taxpayers and that means we pay you, so as your employer I'm revoking you off that sofa and out of this house."

The startled government men left without saying good-bye. Paulie took another swig of beer, a glowing look of contentment on his face. Rocky patted him on the shoulder as he walked toward the kitchen. He met Adrian in the hallway heading in the opposite direction, her arms full of pressed linen.

"Thanks for standing up for me in there."

"Rocky, I don't believe in what you're doing, but they don't have a right to stop you, either."

Then she was gone before he could say anything more. He was getting tired of this avoidance number of hers, but he didn't know what to do about it short of canceling the fight. And that he wouldn't do.

Entering the kitchen, Rocky saw his son staring sullenly at the bowl of Jell-O. Several banana peels were nearby on the counter.

"What's wrong?"

"Uncle Paulie made me put bananas in it. I hate bananas."

Rocky put a comforting arm around his son's small shoulders.

"Yeah ... sometimes life can be kinda rough."

Especially when you're a snowball in hell, he thought.

Rocky was working the speed bag. *Rat-tat-tat*. He enjoyed losing himself in the rhythm of it. *Rat-tat-tat*. Body over mind. He was jarred out of his reverie by flashbulbs suddenly popping nearby. Two excited spectators rushed back to the bleachers, the Polaroid shots already sliding out the bottom of their cameras. They looked with pleasure at the sickly green exposures.

Duke looked at his stopwatch. "Time! Let's get in three rounds on the heavy bag."

As they walked over to the heavy bag Paulie, wearing a T-shirt with printing declaring A VERY IMPORTANT PERSON, wiped the sweat off Rocky with a towel.

"Yo, I can't stand all these people eyeballing. How about you?" he asked Rocky.

Rocky was breathing heavily.

"You talk to Adrian lately?"

"Hey, she's weirding out. If I was you I'd mark a day

on the calendar, like every two weeks, and give her a crack in the mouth. That teaches."

"Teaches what?"

"Respect, pal."

"You got a very twisted personality, Paulie. Y'know, she's gonna have another kid."

"No."

"Yeah."

"When do you get the time?" Paulie asked.

Just then a group of older men wearing olive drab overseas caps festooned with military medals approached. They were obviously World War II veterans from the local V.F.W. The leader of the group stepped forward.

"Rocky, some of the local vets would like to give you this here"—he handed Rocky a hat similar to the ones they were wearing—"and we hope you knock the hell out of him for America and the Veterans of Foreign Wars."

"Thanks, but I'm—" Rocky attempted to object, but nobody was listening to him.

"Let's have a picture with you," the vet continued. "Bob, use your camera."

Suddenly Rocky was surrounded by the smiling old men. He couldn't help but wonder how accurate their memories of war were. He looked at the overseas cap. When opened it had a crease that ran the length of the top. It was similar to the popular Russian hat. The irony wasn't lost on Rocky.

Paulie watched, his eyes full of empathy, as Rocky posed, a smile frozen on his face.


There were more fans waiting outside the gate when they arrived home. It was the same: flags, cheering, the usual platitudes. Rocky was beginning to understand how wars got started.

"And I thought I had a lotta pressure," Paulie said. Paulie would have been hard put to specify what that pressure was, but he bore it gracefully.

Rocky stared straight ahead, the same smile frozen on his lips, his eyes vacant. People raised their cameras.

Pop. Click. Pop. Click.


Adrian woke up to discover that she was alone in the bed. She slipped on a robe and went out into the darkened house. A light glowed from Rocky's study. She went to it like a ship to a beacon.

Rocky was taking down all his awards and trophies when she entered the room.

"Rocky?"

"Yeah?" He turned around, startled.

"What are you doing?" she asked, moving to his side.

"I'm just putting this stuff away."

She glanced at the boxes that were already filled with memorabilia.

"Why?"

"They remind me of things, y'know, that I did in the past. I just wanna think about what I gotta do now."

"You don't have to do anything."

A long pause.

"I gotta leave here." He saw the look of concern on her face. "I can't get ready here. Too many things interrupting—"

"Then find another gym."

"It's not the gym. It's here. I gotta get all this off my mind."

"All this? You mean your family?"

Silence greeted her question. Rocky put some more awards in a box.

"Where are you going?" she asked quietly.

"They're gonna let me train in Russia. I wanna train where there's nobody I know."

That could be here, she thought, because I hardly know you anymore.

"Rocky, don't do this. Give it some time."

"I don't have much time."

"You're not the only one who lives with hurt. Lots of people do."

"A lotta people don't have a choice. I do."

"And for that you're willing to risk everything!" she said angrily.

"I can't live feeling like I do inside. I gotta get it out."

"You're the one who's keeping this revenge thing going! When Apollo fought it wasn't for vengeance, it was for a cause. Rocky, please don't do this to yourself. After all the hell you've been through, you'd think you would have had enough. If you don't care about me, care about your son and the baby."

He put his hands on her shoulders. "I do care. I care about all of you."

She put her arms around his waist. "Then don't throw it all away. Before there were reasons for fighting that I could understand, but I can't understand this. Because even if you win, what have you won? Apollo's still gone. Why can't you change your way of thinking? Everyone else does."

They were at the same impasse they had reached many times before: the big *why*.

"'Cause I'm a fighter. I didn't ask to be one, but that's what I am. That's what you married. We can't change what we really are. You can change the outside, but not the inside."

She felt so frustrated that she wanted to scream, but she was afraid she might not be able to stop. Calm down, she thought, use logic, reasoning. You love him. That's the most important part. You even love his stubbornness.

"But you can't win. You've seen what he can do. You've read what the papers say. Everyone thinks it's suicide."

Rocky wondered what had happened to the even money odds the sportscaster had mentioned at the gym. Pretty soon he'd be accused of being a lemming.

"No, I can't beat Drago on speed, on power, on nothing, Adrian. The only thing I can do is take everything he's got and ask for more. 'Cause to beat me he's gonna have to kill me and to do that he has to have the heart to stand in front of me—to do that he has to be willing to die himself. Is he?"

Rocky threw the last trophy into the box. It shattered. Rocky stalked out of the room.

Adrian picked the pieces of the trophy out of the box and put them back together, her hands shaking. They formed the figure of a boxer, his arms cocked in the ready position.

Rocky sat at the edge of his son's bed. It was early in the morning, but Rocky Junior was wide awake. Rocky was dressed in a suit with an overcoat draped on his arm. Traveling clothes.

"Are you scared?" Rocky Junior asked.

"No."

"Maybe a little?"

125

"The truth is, sometimes I get scared, and I'm so beat up and tired that I'm hoping the other guy knocks me out so it will all go away. But there's another part of me that's not scared, that wants to go another round, 'cause going that one more round when you don't think you can is what will make the difference in your life." He stroked his son's head. He had fine, soft hair like his mother. "When you get older you might need to do something that everybody else thinks is wrong. But it'll be right for you. And you've got to do it. Understand?"

Rocky Junior nodded.

"And remember, Daddy loves you more than anything in the world. Always remember that, okay?"

"Okay."

Rocky Junior fought back his tears as he hugged his father.

Adrian was waiting for him at the bottom of the stairs.

"Well, I guess this is it," Rocky said.

"I can't make you stay?"

Rocky slowly shook his head no, then pulled her into his arms and kissed her. She didn't want to let go. She wanted him here where he belonged.

Paulie yelled from the driveway, "C'mon! The meter's running."

"I love you," Rocky said.

"Oh, Rocky, don't go. Please don't."

"Remember, once I told you I'd never ask you to stop being a woman. Don't ask me to stop being a man."

The look on his face told her she was defeated. No amount of pleading would make any difference. She didn't want his last memory of her to include tears streaming down her cheeks.

"I love you, too," she said bravely.

They walked out of the house, down to the waiting limousine. Paulie finished arguing with the driver about the luggage, telling him to be careful with the plaid ones because they were his. He walked over to his sister and kissed her, then got into the limo.

Rocky kissed Adrian again and followed Paulie into the car.

She watched the limo drive into the early morning mist. The gate opened and closed. They were gone.

All Adrian could think of was the broken statuette of the boxer.

# Chapter 16

The massive 747 banked and came in low over the city
of Leningrad on its descent into the airport. Rocky looked
out the window. He had a good view of the city. Before
leaving the States he had read up on it. It was built by
Peter the Great and originally named after him: St. Peters-
burg. Later it was called Petrograd and now Leningrad.
Rocky could see the sunlight glistening off the ice on the
great Neva river. The city was surrounded by the many
arms of the Neva. It was one of the youngest of the world's
great cities. Also one of the farthest north, situated at
approximately the same latitude as Anchorage, Alaska.

Paulie looked over Rocky's shoulder. It looked cold
down there. Some of the buildings seemed to have gold
domes. Paulie didn't know it, but he was looking at some
of the most historic buildings in Russia: the Smolny mon-
astery, The Peter and Paul Fortress, St. Isaac's Cathedral,
the Church of the Saviour-of-the-Spilled-Blood. It just
looked damned cold to him. And he was right—it was
cold.

Duke saw the snow and ice, too. This was no place
for a boy from Georgia. Of course, Philadelphia hadn't
seemed that hospitable when he had first moved there,
so he would keep an open mind. An eerie feeling crept
through him as he realized that this must have been how
Drago and his wife felt when they landed in New York.

He almost felt sympathy for them until he thought of Apollo.

When they got off the plane they were immediately greeted by a pair of government officials who bore a striking resemblance, in tone if not in visage, to Holmes and Griffin. Rocky and Paulie joked about it, but neither of the officials laughed. Rocky had changed out of his suit in Europe and was now wearing a short, heavy jacket. He looked like what he was going to be: a working man practicing his craft. Paulie was wearing a thick, worn insulated jacket with the words "National Rifle Association" and a flag embroidered on the back. As soon as the cold blasted him he put on a pair of dirty white earmuffs, quickly sheltering them with a Philadelphia Eagles wool watch cap. Duke shivered under his heavy sheepskin jacket.

"This is Russia, huh?" Paulie pondered in his own inimitable way. "It don't look so tough to me."

"It better be Russia. I'm tired of planes," Rocky said, giving Paulie a closer inspection. "You swiped Adrian's earmuffs, didn't you?"

"They look better on me," Paulie said defensively.

"You just put 'em on and they already look dirty."

Paulie took them off and looked at them. Rocky was right. What had happened? Hell, dirty or clean, they were warm. He put them back on.

"How you feeling, Duke?"

"Good, Rocky, but cold, man."

The officials led them through an exit where they were greeted by more officials standing by a highly polished black Mercedes with a staff flag of some kind flying from the fender on the driver's side.

The most official-looking of the officials stepped forward.

"Mr. Balboa?" he inquired.

Paulie almost burst out laughing. Who were they expecting? There weren't that many people trying to get into Russia.

Rocky merely said, "Yeah."

"We will take you to your quarters now. Your bags will be brought after they have been cleared. Please get in."

129

"Guy sounds like Dracula's brother," Paulie whispered to Rocky.

An assistant opened the back car door. Rocky and company climbed in.

Hello, Mother Russia.

The car circled the city and continued into the white countryside, snow and more snow with an occasional bare tree sticking up like a desolate angel. Finally they turned off the road and pulled up to a farmhouse with an adjacent barn. Isolated didn't begin to describe the place, Duke thought. A second car immediately parked behind them, but nobody got out of it.

After they left their car the official proudly swung his arm in a gesture encompassing both buildings. "Like you requested, yes?"

Rocky nodded.

Paulie's eyes bugged out. "You asked for this dump?"

"Yeah," Rocky answered.

"Why? You plan on growing potatoes or something?"

"I just wanna be away from things."

"What a depressing vacation," Paulie groaned. He had a premonition that this was a free trip he was really going to pay for.

"The equipment you requested is in the barn"—the official pointed to the right—"this way."

Paulie was thankful for the directions. Both buildings looked like barns to him.

As they walked to the barn Rocky asked the official about the two men seated in the car.

"They are assigned to you," the official said smugly, "as official chaperons. Where you go, they go. It is okay?"

Rocky shrugged acceptance. He wasn't going anywhere for a while. If they wanted to freeze in a car, let them.

The assistant opened the barn door and the men entered.

Rocky didn't know what he had been expecting, but it was a little more than this. This was just a barn. There had been no attempt to renovate it into a training gym. They had merely hung up a heavy bag, a speed bag, and a double end bag. The air inside was stagnant and oppressive, still tainted with the smell of livestock and their discards. The floor had been swept, but not well. You could still gather up enough hay to make a bale. Shafts of light from high ventilation windows provided dim illumination.

"I'm having a bad dream," Paulie groaned. This was worse than being cleaned out in Las Vegas.

"It's okay?" the official asked.

"We need more light," Duke said.

The official smiled proudly and, like a magician pulling a rabbit out of his hat, flicked a switch on the wall beside him. Naked light bulbs were strung along the interior perimeter of the barn like a string of bizarre Christmas lights. They glowed brightly. In total light the barn looked worse.

"Very modern, yes?" the official beamed.

"It's okay," Rocky said.

"Okay for a retarded reindeer," Paulie commented. "This is beneath human standards here. Complain, will ya? We'll crack out of here."

Rocky ignored him as he continued to inspect the barn.

"When do the sparring partners get here?" Duke asked.

"I do not understand. We provide no sparring partners."

"We were supposed to have them," Duke pushed.

"This I don't know, but you have everything I have been instructed to provide. We are done, yes?" The official looked questioningly at Rocky.

"Yeah."

"What about sparring?" Paulie asked. "I mean, I'd spar with ya, but I might lose control."

"We don't need it." Rocky's voice was firm.

They left the barn and walked toward the house. The two secret service men still sat in the car, silently watching everything. Rocky locked eyes momentarily with the one in the driver's seat. It was like trying to stare down Paulie's robot. Rocky continued toward the house.

They had been assigned a caretaker, Fyodor, and a housekeeper, Anna. They were both in their fifties, friendly, and courteous. The house itself was more comfortable and spacious than it appeared from the outside. Everyone had his own bedroom; there was an interior bathroom with a tub but no shower.

Their luggage arrived and was put in their rooms. His duties completed, the official and his assistant left. But the secret service car remained, an ominous shadow against the pristine white snow.

When Rocky stepped outside the house he was in a sweat suit covered by his heavy jacket, and he wore heavy duty work boots. The secret service men were standing by their car. Paulie and Duke reluctantly stepped out into the cold air. Paulie looked at the men by the car.

"Don't those bums ever get tired?" Paulie asked.

"They're just doing their job." Rocky turned to Duke. "We better get started."

He began to jog down the roadway.

"Start what?" Paulie was confused. "No sparring, no nothing. How can he train like this?"

"'Cause what he's gotta train don't need sparring. He's gotta train what's in here"—Duke thumped his heart with a mitten hand—"to not care."

The secret service car followed Rocky down the roadway keeping the same steady pace he did.

Paulie slept by the fireplace, headphones from a portable cassette player straddling his head, the music blaring into his unconscious ears. Anna had turned out to be a great cook. Her first meal had begun with an assortment of hot and cold hors d'oeuvres—smoked and pickled fish, caviar, vegetable and meat salads—followed by *solianka* soup and a main course of baked salmon, and concluding with huge dishes of ice cream. Paulie had been in pig heaven. Anna considered his heavy snores high praise.

Duke played a silent game of chess with Fyodor. In a half hour neither had spoken more than two words, they were so intent on the game. Fyodor was checked now and pondering how to get out of it. He slid his piece into a new position. Duke smiled and made his final move, trapping Fyodor with his queen.

"Checkmate, friend." Duke smiled.

Fyodor gave a friendly shake of his head and returned the smile.

Duke looked at the closed door of Rocky's bedroom.

* * *

Rocky snipped off a length of tape and applied it to Adrian's picture, which he was holding against the mirror over his sink. He did the same with Rocky Junior's picture. Then he taped a picture of their house next to the other two. He looked fondly at the three pictures crowded in the upper right corner of the mirror. He picked up a fourth photograph. His face turned grim. He taped the picture in the upper left corner of the mirror. It was Drago.

Someone knocked on his door. Rocky opened it. Duke leaned in.

"Rock, can I come in?"

"Sure."

Duke entered the room. He immediately noticed the photographs, but he didn't mention them.

"Some weather up here."

"Yeah," Rocky agreed.

"But for what you got to do it's good. Toughen ya up."

Rocky went to the window and stared out. It was obvious that he had other things on his mind.

"I just wanna say I know you gotta do 'most everything alone up here, and we'll let you be," Duke continued. "But I wanna say that you being here is no accident. Everything has a reason—good or bad, it has a reason. Apollo was like my little brother. I raised him, and when he died a big part of me died. Now you're the one who's gonna keep his spirit alive; you're the one who's gonna make sure he didn't die for nothing. The hell you gotta go through will be harder than anything you ever dreamed, but in the end I know you'll be the one standing."

Except for the eulogy it was the longest speech Duke had ever made. He felt self-conscious but glad that he had said it.

Rocky turned from the window and smiled, but then his vision slid over to the photograph of Drago and the smile vanished.

Rocky's training was as basic and as arduous as the land that surrounded him. He became a familiar figure to the neighboring farmers as he ran across the barren flatlands. The secret service car always followed him. It became as tiring for them as it was for Rocky. The weather was bitter cold, and gusts of wind would rip through him like small knives. He understood how this land had smashed the Nazi army during World War II. It was a tough land that gave birth to tough people. Being tough was the only way they could survive. His respect for the people he encountered during his daily runs grew just as steadily as his body was hardening.

Ludmilla watched Drago running on a treadmill in the sterile confines of his gym. Rimsky and Koloff were confident, but she had been reading the daily reports of Rocky's activities, and they worried her. He seemed to be drawing his strength from the land while Drago was being directed further into scientific technology.

Rocky chopped away at the tree. Each swing of the ax sent chips of wood flying. Despite the cold, sweat flowed freely down his face. The secret service men slapped their arms across their chests to keep warm. Rocky continued to swing relentlessly, each ax blow biting deeper into the tree. The secret service men thought he was crazy, but every day they continued their surveillance of him their respect for him grew. He became *their* crazy man.

Rocky circled the tree and started chopping from the other side. The chips started to pile up on the snow around the tree as the ax continued to swing in a steady, determined rhythm. Finally the tree started to groan. Rocky lowered his ax and pushed the tree gently with one hand. The tree toppled, sending up an explosion of snow. The secret service men went up to Rocky and introduced themselves. The tall one was Anton, the fat one was Leo. Rocky took off his gloves and they shook hands.

Paulie didn't like the beer in Russia at all. You had to open four cases before you found a bottle that wasn't flat. Fyodor went out and got Paulie a plastic bag of kvass, a near beer made by fermenting potatoes. Paulie looked suspiciously at the cloudy contents of the plastic while Fyodor poured some into a glass. He warned Paulie that he had never known a foreigner who had developed a taste for kvass. Undaunted, Paulie took a mouthful. It wasn't bad. It just needed a little kick. Paulie poured some vodka into the plastic bag and sloshed the contents around. He poured some more into his glass and took another swig. He swallowed, grimaced, and coughed. Perfect.

Fyodor looked at him in astonishment, then poured himself a glass. His eyes lit up as he tasted the concoction. Paulie wondered if it was possible to get bananas in Russia during the winter.

The stones were heavy, but Rocky continued to pick them up and pile them into an old, formerly horse-drawn sled. After an hour the sled was full. Anton and Leo watched him with avid curiosity. First trees, now this. They didn't know much about boxing, but they sensed that these were unusual training methods. Rocky hitched himself up to the harness and pulled. Nothing. The sled was frozen to the spot. Rocky took a deep breath and pulled harder, his face turning crimson with the effort. There was a cracking sound as the sled broke loose from the ice. Straining, Rocky walked forward pulling the incredibly heavy sled behind him.

A log fire glowed in the corner of the barn. Rocky pounded away at the heavy bag. Duke and the bag bucked with each blow. The log fire turned the barn into a sweatbox. A right, a left, a right. Duke hung on as blow after blow steadily tore into the heavy bag. Both men were perspiring freely, but neither of them seemed to notice it.

The hill loomed in front of Rocky like a minor mountain. It was about a hundred yards high and pitched at a forty-five degree angle. Rocky's face was windburned. Ice had formed on his eyebrows and on the strands of hair that hung beneath his wool cap. He started pulling the rock-laden sled up the hill. Each step was agony. His muscles felt as if they were going to burst. A quarter of the way up the hill he collapsed, and the sled slid back to the bottom. Leo and Anton rushed up to Rocky. He sat up in the snow, looked at the sled, then up at the hilltop. The secret service men followed his gaze, then looked at each other. No way.

Rocky removed the picture of his house from the mirror and put it in his suitcase. He stared at the photographs of Adrian and Rocky Junior, then turned off the lamp and went to bed.

* * *

Drago pulled the padded arms of the Nautilus-type exercise equipment together in front of him. He relaxed and let the machine pull his arms apart again. He repeated the exercise. Rimsky looked at the computer, carefully checking the pulse and blood pressure readouts. Drago's blond hair was almost invisible against the bleached white walls of the gym.

Rocky strained against the sled harness. His feet were slipping in the snow, but he continued to pull, his eyes fixed on the hilltop. He was halfway up the hill when his legs started to buckle. He gripped the harness tighter and struggled to move his legs. They collapsed under him. The sled flew down the hill, dragging Rocky after it. He looked like a snowball when he landed at the bottom of the hill. Anton and Leo looked at each other. Maybe.

Rocky jumped rope, running backward and forward while spinning. Duke kept a careful eye on the stopwatch. Rocky went faster and faster. He became a blur.

Rocky took down the photos of Adrian and Rocky Junior. After a last lingering look they joined the picture of the house. Rocky shut the suitcase, then returned to the mirror. The only photograph left was of Drago. Rocky stared at it, his eyes hard and merciless.

Rocky was back in harness. The sled had passed the halfway mark on the hillside. Sweat was blinding Rocky, but he continued to pull. He knew where the hilltop was; he didn't have to see it. Step by torturous step he continued upward. His lungs were on fire. The cords of his neck were bulging like cobras preparing to attack. He shut his mind to everything but the next step, then the next one. He was inching toward the top. Left foot, right foot. It reverberated in his mind like a nursery rhyme. Left foot, right foot, turn yourself about. The pain in his muscles was so intense it was almost pleasurable. Left foot, right foot. The sled moved upward with each jerk. Suddenly all sensation left Rocky—no pain, no cold, no fire in the lungs. He had passed all those thresholds. Two more steps and he couldn't feel the weight of the sled. What's happening? he thought. He dropped the harness and turned around.

He was at the top of the hill! He had done it! The secret service men looked considerably smaller from his vantage point. He pushed the sled over on its side and sent it tumbling down the hill, rocks flying wildly. Anton and Leo started to run back to the car.

"DRAGOOOOOOOOOOO!" Rocky yelled in a voice loud enough to start an earthquake. The yell echoed down the mountain as the sled rolled over and over, breaking apart until it was just a mass of splintered wood.

Rocky jogged back to the house. Leo and Anton followed at a longer than usual distance. The display with the sled had made them a little nervous. Some of the rocks had hit the car. One window was cracked. Maybe Rocky wasn't so crazy.

As Rocky approached the house, the door opened. Adrian stepped out, beautiful in a fur coat and hat.

They were stunned by each other's appearance. Rocky thought she was the most gorgeous woman he had ever seen. She was startled by the hardened, worn expression on his face. For a few seconds they just stared at each other. Then Rocky walked to her, almost timidly.

"I couldn't stay away any more."

Rocky nodded and moved closer, his expression still the same.

"I missed you so much," Adrian continued, her voice low and gentle.

"I missed you, too."

"I'm with you no matter what."

"No matter what?" Rocky asked, his expression softening.

"No matter what," she repeated firmly.

He took her in his arms. She seemed so light and fragile. He tenderly bent down and kissed her. She hugged him ferociously.

Leo and Anton observed.

# Chapter 17

It snowed in Leningrad on Christmas day. Not the light, fluffy kind of snow that children like to play around in—this was the heavy kind that piled up on the ground so fast that it became hard to walk through. It could ensnarl your legs, trap you. This was the kind of snow that had broken the back of the German army during World War II. They had laid siege to the city for over nine hundred days and discovered that they were the ones who were captured. By the snow.

By evening there were six inches of new snow on the ground, but it didn't deter the people of Leningrad. They prided themselves on being a hardy bunch. In fact, they prided themselves on a lot of things: their museums, their palaces, the more than three hundred bridges that crossed the Neva. Other Russians found them downright smug. Stalin had hated them. But they survived him, just as they had the Germans. They didn't mind the snow. It was part of their heritage. They merely bundled themselves up in heavy winter clothing and walked to the newly erected sports arena. There was to be a fight between the Russian champion and the American champion. They wanted to see it. A lot of them wanted to see it. The snow by the arena entrance was trampled as flat as freshly cut grass. And people were still filing in.

Inside, the arena was jammed and hot. People were

sitting on coats and jackets. Most of the spectators were Russians. A few third world people were scattered about the crowd. Huge posters of Soviet leaders, past and present, hung from the ceiling. Stalin and Kruschev were not represented. The largest poster was of Lenin. He looked down on the crowd with a fierce but fatherly expression. Various flags bearing Soviet symbols hung from the walls. The largest of these, a massive red flag with the Soviet hammer and sickle on it, was stretched across the private box that contained high Soviet officials including the premier. He looked at the poster of Lenin enviously. He hoped he would have that staying power.

An air of excitement and anticipation emanated from the audience. Russia was not famous for its nightlife and probably never would be. An event like this would be remembered for a long time. The spectators continued to pour in. The arena was filled to the point of bursting.

At ringside it was like a small United Nations. Commentators from a variety of countries were present: Japan, Nicaragua, England, Germany, France, and, of course, the United States and Russia.

Halburn and White had drawn the lucky duty of representing the U.S.A. They had covered the fight with the Russian in Las Vegas, so some television executive had decided they would have more insight into the fight tonight. They didn't argue. It was an assignment commentators would kill for.

Halburn stared straight into the portable television camera.

"Well, good evening, ladies and gentlemen from around the world, and welcome to what will be the most widely watched ring battle in history. The Iron Horse, the Italian Stallion from America, Rocky Balboa, is taking on the Siberian Express, Ivan Drago, in what has been touted as a mini-World War III."

Vega finished taping Drago's hands while Rimsky massaged his back. Koloff entered the dressing room flanked by a KGB agent. He strode over to Drago. Rimsky and Vega suddenly found other duties to perform. Koloff was alone with Drago.

"Tonight is the night we have been working toward for over twenty years. Your victory will bring us great glory and you will be well rewarded," Koloff said, genuine excitement in his voice. "Disgrace him!"

Drago silently turned toward the mirror and started snapping lightning-fast punches at his reflection. He didn't need Koloff to tell him what to do. He was after destruction, not disgrace.

Rocky's back and arms were being greased by Paulie. The lubricant was shiny and slippery. Rocky's face had already been greased. Paulie ended by running his slick hands around the inside of the waistband of Rocky's shorts, assuring that they wouldn't rub against his skin. Every little advantage counted.

Adrian opened the door and looked in.

"It'll be alright," Rocky assured her.

"I know it will." She smiled tightly and left.

Paulie wiped his hands on a towel.

"Yo, Rocko—"

"Yeah."

"Listen, I wanna tell you something I never told you," Paulie said earnestly, looking uncomfortable. He seemed to be squirming around inside his clothes. "I know I act stupid sometimes and say stupid things, but you give me respect. . . . It's hard to say these things 'cause I'm not this way, but if I could unzip myself and step out and be somebody else, I'd wanna be you. . . . You're all heart, Rocko."

"Thanks, Paulie," Rocky said tersely. Paulie wasn't the only one for whom the speech had been uncomfortable.

"Smack this creep's teeth out, okay?" Paulie added.

Rocky nodded.

He left Duke and Paulie and went into the lavatory. They understood. This was a ritual of his. He knelt by the commode and tried to pray. Nothing came to mind. All he thought of was Apollo being smashed into the mat, the whirring noise as the casket was lowered into the ground. He didn't have any thoughts he wanted to exchange with God. He stood up and looked into the mirror. He wasn't sure he recognized himself.

Back at home Rocky Junior and a gang of friends were grouped around the television set. They were a pushing, squirming, noisy mass. They were kids. Mrs. Tulio had set a bowl of popcorn on the floor and they devoured it while they kept their eyes on the television.

Rocky Junior had the most prominent spot, smack in front of the set.

"Does anybody want to bet?" he asked.

Shades of Paulie.

Ringside was a battle of languages as all the commentators tried to communicate with their audiences. White and Halburn, being veteran announcers, had an advantage—they could really yell.

"Rumor has it Rocky trained himself for this fight, but as strong as he may be his strength is certainly dwarfed by Drago's massiveness."

White confirmed his partner's opinion. "Drago's power is without question, as evidenced by the tragedy of Apollo Creed. Balboa may be ready, but with speed, age, and size against him most experts have Balboa on the losing end. It's already been noted that this is the most widely viewed sporting event in recent history, but that's an understatement. Streets here and in America are virtually empty."

Suddenly the sounds of booing and whistling drowned out the commentary. The crowd was on its feet. Rocky walked down the aisle toward the ring. Duke and Paulie flanked him. Security guards surrounded all three. The crowd continued to roar its disapproval.

"One of the fighters—I think—yes, it's the ex-champ—Rocky Balboa is making his way down to the ring.... Listen to this crowd!"

The boos had given way to jeers and crude gestures.

"We knew he wouldn't be popular, but this borders on pure hatred, folks!" Halburn exclaimed.

Rocky walked through the crowd, his eyes straight ahead. If he heard them, he gave no indication. Paulie watched him protectively. Rocky just continued walking as if he were in a trance.

"Rocky's face is like stone. It seems the booing crowd has no effect on his concentration."

Rocky glanced up at the huge red flag hanging from the dignitaries' box. Just by chance the premier was looking down at him. They locked eyes momentarily.

"The ex-champ has a look tonight that could burn through lead."

As Rocky passed Halburn and White and climbed into the ring the booing escalated.

"This crowd sounds insane," White yelled.

"It has to be bothering the ex-champ," Halburn insisted.

"If it is, he's not showing it. I've never seen such tension at a sporting event."

Rocky was in his corner limbering up, shaking his muscles loose. Paulie put a paper sack he was carrying on the floor, then climbed up to join Rocky. Duke looked curiously at the bag, then followed Paulie.

The arena erupted into more noise, but this time it was cheering. Drago walked down the opposite aisle, Rimsky and Vega by his side. The crowd went wild. A band situated below the dignitaries' box struck up the Russian national anthem. Everyone stood up.

Drago stopped and waited until the music was finished, then continued toward the ring. He was a towering structure of confidence. He looked up at the dignitaries' box and gave a slight bow of respect. The premier saluted him. Rocky watched Drago's procession, his eyes tightening in anticipation.

Drago climbed into the ring and glared at Rocky as he gracefully shook his muscles loose.

All the sportscasters suddenly came alive, especially the Russian commentator. He seemed to be eating his microphone. Paulie wondered what he was saying.

Rocky and Drago paced up and down the ring in their robes, glaring at each other like two wild animals.

"Look at those expressions," Halburn commented. "This is like waiting for a volcano to explode."

"It sure is."

Paulie rubbed the back of Rocky's robe.

"You're going all the way tonight, Rocko."

"All the way," Rocky growled, each word sounding fiercer than the preceding one.

The spectators at the rear of the arena started to chant. As the sound rolled through the audience it gained momentum and volume until, when it finally reached the ring, it was a tidal wave of noise: DRAGO DRAGO DRAGO DRAGO. It continued, wave after wave assault-

142

ing the arena. The walls seemed to reverberate with the chant.

Drago waved to the crowd and removed his robe. He looked like a blond skyscraper. On the corner of his dark maroon trunks was the Russian symbol of the hammer and sickle. More cheering.

Rocky bounced up and down on the balls of his feet, his eyes never leaving the Russian. He reminded Duke of Apollo at Las Vegas. Duke wiped the thought from his mind.

The bell rang. The referee summoned the fighters to the center of the ring with a wave of his hands. Paulie stuck close to Rocky as they walked to the referee. Drago advanced boldly with Rimsky by his side.

The referee spoke in Russian, but Rocky didn't need an interpreter. He had heard the litany before, maybe too often.

"Fight clean, break clean—"

"Tonight's your night," Paulie said, trying to combat the endless chanting that still washed down from the audience.

Rocky was impervious to it all. He and Drago were toe-to-toe, silently assaulting each other with psychological weapons. If looks could kill . . .

"Go to a neutral corner after a knockdown." The referee touched their gloves together. "Now fight."

"Try speaking American," Paulie said to the uncomprehending referee.

Drago glared at Rocky. "I will break you."

"Go for it," Rocky said, his eyes never wavering.

They both continued to stare as they returned to their corners.

Drago gripped the ropes and did knee bends while Rimsky delivered instructions in Russian. From here on in the only time any of the Russians would use English would be when addressing Rocky.

"The world is watching. You must beat him. You must disgrace him!"

Drago wasn't listening. His eyes searched the ringside audience until he saw Ludmilla. Koloff was once again sitting beside her. She smiled. Drago's face didn't change expression, but she knew.

Rocky twisted his neck, shaking any kinks out, while

Paulie loosened the belt of his robe.

Duke kept chanting in Rocky's ear: "You're the man, Rock. There's no better. Do what you came here to do. Do it. You're the man. . . ."

Rocky nodded, his eyes fastened on Adrian sitting in her front row seat. Their eyes silently locked for a moment that was just theirs.

Paulie took the robe off Rocky. Underneath he wore Apollo's red, white, and blue trunks in one last tribute to the master showman. Duke's eyes misted over and he took a deep breath. The satin trunks gleamed in the bright ring lights, a magical, living flag.

The crowd roared an angry disapproval.

"Now we know one thing," Rocky said.

"What?" Duke asked.

"Nobody here is color-blind."

Rocky instinctively dropped to one knee and made the sign of the cross.

Across the ring, Drago smirked in disdain.

The bell rang. Round one.

Rocky fired out of his corner determined to take the fight immediately to the big Russian, but Drago kept circling to the right, flashing stiff jabs that succeeded in keeping Rocky off balance. Every time he'd move in for the body he'd find Drago's glove in his face. Rocky was connecting, but not as effectively as he wanted. He had the feeling Drago was playing cat and mouse with him. Suddenly the Russian's jabs turned into right- and left-hand bombs. They were landing. Rocky could hear a ringing sound in his head. He knew he had to do something quickly.

"Rocky comes firing from his corner, but is met with stiff opposition. The Russian, with his massive reach, is keeping the Philly Slugger off balance."

"Go after him, Rocko!" Paulie screamed from the corner.

Rocky went. He leapt up and cracked Drago with a murderous right. A jolt of pleasure ran down Rocky's arm. The Russian merely shrugged it off and smirked. It was like a bug splattering on a car window. The crowd roared for its hero.

"Rocky just pulverized Drago with a leaping hook—" Halburn interrupted. "And Drago just smiled."

The arrogant smile made Rocky lose control. He attacked the Russian with a vengeance. He threw jabs and combinations, trying to fill the bases and set up a grand slam home run, but all he was hitting was air. The Russian was fast. It was like having a redwood tree vanish before your eyes.

Adrian felt her stomach twisting into a knot. An ominous feeling started to flood her. She hoped it didn't show on her face.

The cheers from the audience grew louder. As if drawing energy from the rabid crowd, Drago responded with a powerhouse left jab that caught Rocky off guard and staggered him. The Russian instantly followed up with a series of combinations that left Rocky wavering like the top of a tree in a storm.

The spectators jumped to their feet. They sensed blood, American blood.

Adrian was standing, too.

"Back up! Back up!" she yelled, but her voice was lost in the din of the crowd.

Paulie and Duke were frantically yelling instructions even though they knew Rocky couldn't hear them.

"Christ, tie him up!"

"Move! Keep moving!"

White's voice was filled with excitement. "Rocky's hurt! He woke up the giant and he's paying the price!"

A right connected above Rocky's eye. Blood spurted, then oozed.

"He's cut, too!"

Rocky bobbed and weaved, backpedaled, and circled sideways, but the Russian was always there, connecting, connecting. Another right slipped through Rocky's battered defenses and he floated down to one knee.

People started stamping their feet. The arena was vibrating.

Rocky stood and took the mandatory eight count. He waved to Paulie and Duke that he was all right.

Drago continued attacking. The knockdown had swept the fury from Rocky's mind. He started boxing Apollo's way. He danced the way he had learned in Los Angeles. Step, step, jab. Step, step, jab. It was like a cassette playing in his head. Drago's blows were missing their mark. Each second Rocky got stronger.

Paulie and Duke nodded to each other in approval.

Suddenly a hook connected to Rocky's midsection. The air *whoosh*ed out of him. He bent over. Drago corrected his posture with a right uppercut. Everything was blurry to Rocky. His feet seemed to be tangled up. Somebody had stopped the music to his dance. Two thunderous rights in a row and Rocky hit the canvas.

Rocky was on his feet by the count of seven, but he was dazed. He couldn't even hear the crowd roaring.

"Rocky was smashed to the canvas!"

"But he wants more!"

"Rocky! Stay down!" Adrian screamed.

But he didn't. He pushed the referee away.

Rocky Junior couldn't take his eyes off the television set. Was this really happening to his dad? Was this what boxing was about? It was horrible. He wanted it to end. He wanted his mother and father home.

"Your dad's getting smashed," a friend said quietly.

Rocky Junior blinked, but the picture didn't go away. It was real, not a nightmare.

Rimsky motioned to Drago to move in for the kill. He did, cutting off Rocky's ring space with amazing speed, attempting to corner him. But Rocky miraculously slipped out of the corner and whipped a three-punch combination into Drago's gut.

"Go, Rocko! Beat his ass!" Paulie was jumping up and down.

Rocky sidestepped a whistling hook and drove another series of body blows into Drago. He was beginning to hear the music again.

"Get him!" Adrian yelled.

Rimsky's face contorted into an ugly mask as he screamed, "Defense, you fool! Defense!"

The fact that Rocky was not only standing but actually landing punches made Drago maniacal.

"Don't wait! Attack!" Rimsky screamed, contradicting himself.

Drago wasn't listening to him, but he did attack. It was as if a flurry of computerized frenzy had been unleashed. Drago's blows landed with deadly accuracy. Rocky thought

146

he was in a fist storm, then he felt nothing.

He was on the canvas. It was begining to look familiar to him, even through a blood haze. He grabbed a rope and pulled himself erect.

"The southpaw is in serious trouble. If they don't stop this, someone's going to get killed."

Adrian ran to Paulie. "Stop it, Paulie!"

Paulie hesitated, looking at the towel.

Rocky looked over to his corner and nodded that he was all right. He wasn't, but why make it public?

Duke looked at Paulie and said, "Don't!"

Paulie motioned Adrian back to her seat.

"Destroy him! What's wrong?" Rimsky continued to scream.

Drago was trying to comply. He was hitting Rocky with everything he had. But Rocky wouldn't go down! His legs buckled and his eyes were glassy, but he wouldn't go down.

The bell rang. Rocky hadn't known three minutes could be so long.

Drago glared at him with undiluted hate. "I will kill you!"

Rocky could barely hear him. Paulie and Duke guided him to his seat. Duke worked on his eye while Paulie gave him water and pulled at his waistband to give him air.

"What's going on out there?" Duke demanded.

"He's winning," Rocky panted.

Rimsky stood directly in front of his fighter and harangued him.

"You are not doing as you're told! He is small! He is weak! You are stronger!"

Drago nodded, pushed Rimsky out of the way, and stared at Rocky.

Adrian was on the edge of her chair, lost in a vortex of confusion. It should be stopped, but Rocky didn't want to throw in the towel. She started to rise, reconsidered, and sat back down.

"Stay in his face," Duke counseled. "He'll tire out. He's never been hurt! You hurt him and you'll take his heart. Give him the hurt!"

* * *

The bell rang. Round two.

"There's the bell for round two of this one-sided battle!"

"It will take more than luck for Rocky to survive this round," Halburn said sagely.

But Rocky whipped out of his corner with renewed energy. He couldn't understand it himself, but it was there. He could feel it in his arms and legs.

"Tear him up!" Duke encouraged.

Rocky exploded jabs and hooks into Drago's body. His fists were pounding like perfectly timed pistons. He kept digging into Drago's body, scoring again and again. Startled, Drago backpedaled.

The premier's face showed concern. Automatically, all the other dignitaries' faces showed concern, too.

Drago launched a counterattack, but Rocky dodged the lethal blows and continued to pound away at Drago's body.

"Take his heart, Rocko!" Paulie urged.

The color was returning to Adrian's cheeks.

"Please..." she whispered to herself.

Rocky continued to charge, but a right hand stopped him. He shook it off and bulled ahead. His punches were finding their targets.

"Rocky is tearing holes through the Russian."

Rocky continued to lunge forward, score, and retreat before Drago could counterpunch.

The audience was booing and jeering. It was sweet music to Paulie's ears.

"Chop him down!" he yelled, his face ecstatic.

It was almost as if Paulie's cry gave Drago momentum. His punches began to get through and connect. A sharp left jab set up a long bomber right. Rocky reeled back, exposing a vulnerable solar plexus. Drago's fists found it like homing pigeons. Rocky's arms dropped. Drago fired a series of right-hand bombs that could be heard by the people in the back of the arena. Rocky saw so many sparks he thought flashbulbs were popping. He couldn't see anything else. He was punching blind, but he was still punching.

"Stay with him!"

Duke's voice seemed like a distant memory to Rocky. Even the crowd's angry chorus seemed to be filtered through a sponge. But Rocky stayed with Drago. He was staggering, swaying, bouncing off the ropes, but he was staying with him. He was taking Drago's best and still standing.

"Rocky should be out, but he's fighting back!"

Rocky caught the Russian with a sledgehammer right that opened a gash over the left eye. Now they were both bleeding buckets.

"Lethal punch after punch. Amazing willpower! The Russian is cut! He's cut!"

Drago put his glove to his eye, then stared dazed at his own blood. He had never seen it before. Nobody had ever cut him before. He went berserk. He attacked Rocky like a wild animal. The sheer number and force of the blows drove Rocky back against the ropes. The Russian continued to pummel Rocky, but he couldn't put him down. The slaughter was finally stopped by the bell.

Drago's chest was heaving from exhaustion. His face was twisted by hate. Even Ludmilla found him a fearsome sight.

"I will kill you. . . ." he said very slowly and seriously.

Tell me something new, Rocky thought, then yelled, "Drago!"

The giant fighter glared over his shoulder as he walked back to his corner.

"You're bleeding."

A subtle change swept over the crowd. The noise was as deafening, but the cheers weren't just for Drago—they were for the fight and the sheer, brutal competitiveness of the two fighters.

"Balboa, hurt and tired, took the Russian's best again, but how much punishment can a human being stand?"

Duke started patching up the cut again. Paulie wiped the sweat and blood from Rocky.

"You're doing great, Rock, great. I couldn't do no better, really."

"Thanks."

"He's cut! Cut bad! You got him worried. You hurt him." Duke's words came out in rapid-fire fashion.

But Rocky was beyond words. They meant nothing to him anymore. He twisted his head so he could see Adrian. It helped. He felt better.

\* \* \*

Vega cursed Rimsky in Spanish for getting in the way while the Cuban worked on Drago's eye. It was a nice, dangerous cut.

"How is my eye?"

Rimsky ignored the question. To hell with the eye.

"How can you do this? He is easy for you! To be cut by this man is a disgrace."

"He fights like an animal. How is my eye?"

"He is nothing! He is weak!"

"You are wrong. He is like stone."

Halburn and White couldn't believe the battle they were watching.

"Rocky may be on the receiving end so far, but he's here to fight. This is shaping up into a personal war, and right now it's anybody's fight."

Duke finished with the eye. "You know what you gotta do, so do it, Rock. All the way!"

The bell rang and Rocky stepped into a dream—or a nightmare. The rounds went by in a haze. His arms and legs were moving by instinct. Sometimes he'd give a punch, other times he'd receive. It hardly mattered any more. The main thing was to keep going.

The premier was no longer concerned, he was worried. Deep furrows creased his wide brow.

The crowd began to emotionally identify with Rocky. They had been battered beyond resistance, yet they had resisted. They had been like the tenacious underdog without enough sense to surrender. They had been what Rocky was now.

Adrian and Ludmilla watched, horrified yet fascinated, as their husbands tried to destroy each other. They had the same feelings: revulsion and pride.

Each round brought Rocky more confidence. He was still standing and punching. That was the important thing. He no longer thought beyond the next blow. Survival was all that mattered.

Paulie drove himself into a demonic frenzy as he cheered Rocky on. He couldn't stand still. He felt as if high voltage electricity were flowing through his body. Go, Rocko, go.

Drago couldn't understand it. Balboa wouldn't drop. After years of being told he wasn't human, Drago had finally encountered someone *he* thought wasn't human.

He continued to land blows, but they seemed to have no effect on Balboa. For the first time in his life Drago was tired. His arms were logs, his legs concrete pillars. A deadly weariness was penetrating to the core of him. He had to fight it.

Rocky dropped his arms momentarily and the Russian fired off a right-hand missile that erupted flush on Rocky's chin. Rocky staggered back. Drago pounced on him, hammering with more rights until Rocky was driven into the mat like a nail.

Rocky struggled to his knees and looked up. Drago was glaring down at him. Neither man could see the other distinctly.

The referee pushed Drago to a neutral corner.

One, two, three. It sounded to Rocky as if the referee were counting under water. Or maybe Rocky was the one who was immersed. He floated up to a standing position before the ten count. The referee backed away. Rocky immediately charged the Russian. The startled giant backed up in wonderment. Rocky pulverized him with a flurry of hard-hitting combinations. Pain exploded across Drago's face and body. He staggered and fell back against the ropes. The bell signaled the end of the round.

Dazed, Drago walked back to his corner.

The crowd applauded Rocky as he sank onto his stool.

"This place is ready to explode! An incredible fight with neither man backing off! And Balboa's bravery is actually winning over the crowd."

Rocky sat in his corner, his eyes glazed, not focusing. "What round . . . what round is it?"

"The fifteenth! You're gonna do it. You can win it all. One more round!" Duke urged as he attended to Rocky's wounds.

A murmuring started that swelled into a chant. But this time it was Rocky's name the crowd was yelling.

Adrian turned her head in surprise as she heard the sound: ROCKY ROCKY ROCKY.

Rimsky was incensed. He screamed into his weary fighter's face, "You idiot! I cannot believe this."

"He's not human."

"You had him hurt, you had him down—"

Ludmilla rushed up to the corner. "Drago! Drago! Are you all right?"

Drago nodded wearily.

"Please, you must win!" she urged. "You must win or we all will lose."

"I am trying!"

Koloff pushed Ludmilla out of the way.

"What the hell have you done?" he screamed at Rimsky. "You trained this fool, and he disgraces us!" Koloff turned to Drago. "Listen to that, you bastard. Our people cheer for him. The world is seeing this, you stupid animal. Win! Do you understand? Win!"

Koloff slapped Drago's face.

Ludmilla backed away.

Drago rose slowly from his stool. Koloff suddenly realized what he had done. The color drained from his face. Drago grabbed Koloff by the throat with one hand and lifted him off his feet. Koloff's eyes bulged and his tongue popped out as he choked. Drago tightened his grip.

"No!" Ludmilla screamed.

Drago threw Koloff away like a piece of garbage. Koloff landed on his back.

"After this fight you are finished!" Koloff gasped and looked at Ludmilla. "All of you are finished!"

Drago ignored him and raised his arms to the Soviet premier.

"I win for me! For me and Ludmilla!"

Adrian was back at Rocky's corner. He looked down at her with his bruised and swollen face. She thought he looked beautiful.

"Do it, Rocky! Do it! You can! The whole world is proud of you! I love you! Do it!"

The audience continued to chant: ROCKY ROCKY ROCKY.

"An incredible sight. Rocky's fighting spirit has won the respect of this crowd. Amazing!"

Duke massaged Rocky's shoulders. "You're behind on points. You gotta knock him out to win. You gotta punch and punch till you can't punch no more. This is your whole life here. Get him now!"

The bell sounded. Round fifteen.

The crowd was still chanting. The sound echoed off the walls of the arena. The Soviet premier's face reddened as the chant bombarded him.

The fighters moved to the center of the ring and grudgingly touched gloves.

"I will beat you," Drago growled, "you bastard!"

"The men touch gloves and prepare for one more brutal round. They move cautiously around each other with Rocky moving ahead."

Rocky Junior and his friends had their eyes fixed on the television set. Mrs. Tulio stood behind, another bowl of popcorn in her hands forgotten as she watched the furious fight.

"Daddy, go for it!" Rocky Junior yelled.

Drago was raining blows down on Rocky at will.

"Rocky is just taking punishment and moving ahead, totally exhausted."

The blows continued to come. Rocky huddled in a crouch, his arms pulled into his side protectively, his gloves sheltering his face. He was being knocked from side to side like a heavy bag. He made no attempt to counterpunch. He seemed powerless. Drago was turning him into his personal punching bag.

Paulie and Duke were frantic. "Fight, Rock! What're you waiting for?"

The Soviet premier was smiling now. This was what he had come to see. A feeling of relief swept through the delegation like a cool breeze.

Adrian was standing and yelling, "Rocky, hit him! Hit him!"

"It had to happen. Rocky is absolutely exhausted, taking punch after punch," Halburn said sadly.

"They may have to stop this," White added mournfully.

But the spectators were still with Rocky. The chant grew in intensity until it filled the arena: ROCKY ROCKY ROCKY ROCKY.

Rocky continued to absorb punishment, but he showed no signs of going down. Drago didn't know what to do. It seemed impossible to knock Balboa down. The grim, unrelenting look on Rocky's face was not the look of a defeated man. Rocky began to bore forward. Drago still viciously hammered away with long rights, but their power was failing. He was having a lot of firsts that night, and now came the ultimate one: fear. Drago began to panic.

His cruel expression of hatred faltered.

Rocky knew it was now or never. If he didn't go for it now, there wouldn't be another chance. He heard Apollo whispering in his ear: The eye of the tiger, man, the eye of the tiger. Mickey was on the other side of him: Get mad, get mean, get mad! Rocky exploded off his feet with a sledgehammer right hook into the Russian's jaw. Drago reeled backwards, his eyes wide with disbelief. Rocky jumped on him. Now *he* was the one dropping the bombs, and they were landing. Rocky whipped blow after blow into Drago's midsection. The giant felt a rib cave in. The pain was excruciating, but Drago didn't utter a sound. He could take it as well as give it.

The Russian snapped out a jab that startled Rocky. Drago grabbed the opportunity and turned Rocky into a corner. He pounded away at Rocky with bone-crushing punches. He wanted to break Balboa's ribs, smash them into fine powder.

Rocky slipped a jab and shot a power right-hander over it. Drago was stunned. Rocky followed up with a series of jabs that allowed him to get out of the corner. Now they were both in the center of the ring, standing toe-to-toe, hammering away at each other. All vestiges of the science of boxing were gone. They were just two men beating on each other. No style, no tricks, just guts and stamina. The audience was going insane.

"Technique is gone, strategy is gone, it's just head-to-head warfare. It's just who wants it the most!"

The brutal battle continued. No defense, just a wild swinging of punches. Both men were taking what they were giving. It couldn't go on like this much longer.

Rocky found an opening in Drago's solar plexus. He filled it with a series of excruciating left-right combinations that cracked another of Drago's ribs. This time a groan forced its way out of Drago's lips. Rocky continued to assault the Russian. Drago's legs began to buckle.

"Balboa is chopping the Russian down like a tree!"

In the living room everyone, including Mrs. Tulio, was chanting, "Go for it! Go for it! Go for it!"

Rocky Junior's face was flushed with pride.

\* \* \*

Drago fell back against the ropes as Rocky continued to maim him. Drago's body was a temple of pain. Now his bulk seemed to be working against him. He was a bigger target. Drawing on deep resources he didn't even know he had, Drago managed to get off the ropes and battle back to the center of the ring. But Rocky was relentless. Jabs were followed by right hooks. When Drago raised his hands to protect his face thunderous blows crashed against his injured ribs. His legs didn't seem to work; they wobbled instead of dancing backwards. Rocky lunged forward with a haymaker right that caught Drago square in the jaw, sending him back into the ropes. Another lunge was accompanied by another right hand. Drago didn't know where he was. One last right that started in Philadelphia ended against Drago's nose, broke it, and sent him flying through the ropes, letting Drago know hwere he was. He was in hell. He landed on the floor, flat on his back. He tried to get up but collapsed.

The arena exploded in joyous celebration.

The premier and his contingent unceremoniously exited their box.

Rimsky dropped his towel in disgust and walked away as the crowd surged past him on the way to the ring.

Ludmilla rushed to her husband, her face horror-stricken. Drago was still, his eyes closed. She cradled his head in her arms. His eyes slowly opened.

Adrian was swept up by the crowd as she groped her way to the ring.

"Rocky has done the impossible, and these people love it. It's absolute pandemonium!"

Paulie, Duke, and Rocky were jumping up and down in the center of the ring hugging one another.

"Incredible! You're incredible, man. Look what you did! You made history!" Duke yelled in joy.

Paulie had the paper bag with him.

"I been saving this," he said, taking an American flag out of the bag.

Paulie shook the flag loose. It unfurled, revealing the Stars and Stripes.

Adrian forced her way to Rocky.

"I'm so proud of you." She kissed him.

155

Paulie draped the American flag over Rocky's shoulders.

The fans rushed into the ring and swept Rocky aloft, the red, white, and blue glistening on his shoulders. Behind him the massive red Soviet flag could be seen. Rocky smiled and waved.

Halburn struggled and pushed his way through the cheering crowd, the Russian announcer hot on his heels. Rocky reached down and took the microphone from Halburn.

"Excuse me!" Rocky yelled. "I wanna say something!"

The roar of the crowd began to die down as the Russian announcer translated what Rocky was saying.

"When I came here I didn't know what to expect," Rocky continued. "All I seen is a lotta people hating me and I guess I didn't like you too much neither."

The crowd was stunned into silence.

"My best friend, Apollo Creed, he once said that people can't change—you are what you are. He died."

Adrian looked up at Rocky, pride glistening in her eyes.

"Tonight, I seen a lot of changes in here. I seen two men tryin' to kill each other, but I guess that's better than twenty million. So what I'm tryin' to say to whoever wants to listen is . . . I can change, and you can change—everybody can change!"

The crowd cheered, applauded, and roared in unison.
ROCKY BALBOA!
CHAMPION OF THE WORLD!